GRAMMAR FIRST AID for PRIMARY TEACHERS

GRAMMAR FIRST AID FOR PRIMARY TEACHERS

JO HEFFER

CORWIN

CORWIN
A SAGE Publishing Company

A SAGE company
2455 Teller Road
Thousand Oaks, California 91320
(0800)233-9936
www.corwin.com

SAGE Publications Ltd
1 Oliver's Yard
55 City Road
London EC1Y 1SP

SAGE Publications India Pvt Ltd
B 1/I 1 Mohan Cooperative Industrial Area
Mathura Road
New Delhi 110 044

SAGE Publications Asia-Pacific Pte Ltd
3 Church Street
#10-04 Samsung Hub
Singapore 049483

Editor: Amy Thornton
Senior project editor: Chris Marke
Marketing Manager: Dilhara Attygalle
Cover design: Wendy Scott
Typeset by: C&M Digitals (P) Ltd, Chennai, India

Library of Congress Control Number: 2020936771

British Library Cataloguing in Publication data

A catalogue record for this book is available from the
British Library

ISBN 978-1-5297-3044-9
ISBN 978-1-5297-3043-2 (pbk)

CONTENTS

Acknowledgements   vii
About the author   ix
Introduction   xi

Part 1   The basics: building on KS1 and EYFS   **1**

1.1   Words   3

1.2   Sentences, texts and punctuation   15

Part 2   Teaching grammar in Years 3 and 4   **25**

2.1   A Framework for teaching the Year 3 and 4 statutory requirements   27

2.2   Extending the range of sentences with more than one clause by
      using a wider range of conjunctions, including *when, if, because, although*   31

2.3   Using the present perfect form of verbs in contrast to the past tense   39

2.4   Choosing nouns or pronouns appropriately for clarity and cohesion,
      and to avoid repetition   47

2.5   Using conjunctions, adverbs and prepositions to express
      time and cause   55

2.6 Using fronted adverbials and commas after fronted adverbials   67

2.7 Years 3 and 4 punctuation   75

Part 3   Teaching grammar in Years 5 and 6   **83**

3.1 Years 5 and 6 statutory requirements   85

3.2 Recognising vocabulary and structures that are appropriate for formal
     speech and writing, including subjunctive forms   89

3.3 Using passive verbs to affect the presentation of information in a sentence 99

3.4 Using the perfect form of verbs to mark relationships of time and cause   107

3.5 Using expanded noun phrases to convey complicated information concisely   115

3.6 Using modal verbs or adverbs to indicate degrees of possibility   123

3.7 Using relative clauses beginning with who, which, where, when,
     whose, that or using an implied (i.e. omitted) pronoun   129

3.8 Years 5 and 6 punctuation   137

Part 4   You've taught it but have they learnt it?   **151**

4.1 Assessment   153

Glossary   163
References   167
Index   169

ACKNOWLEDGEMENTS

This book is dedicated to my husband Simon and my daughters, Rachel and Natalie. Thank you for your patience and your belief in me.

It is also dedicated to all the amazing and inspirational teachers that I have worked with and particularly those who attended my training courses and encouraged me to write it.

ABOUT THE AUTHOR

Jo Heffer has worked as a teacher, literacy subject leader and education consultant for 30 years. She currently works part time for Windsor and Maidenhead as an advisor and assessment manager alongside working as an independent literacy consultant. Her passion for literacy has taken her to many parts of England to run successful courses on teaching grammar and punctuation as well as all other aspects of literacy. The overwhelmingly positive response to the training has led to the writing of this book.

INTRODUCTION

This book is a handbook for all primary teachers, especially those teaching in Key Stage 2. It guides you through the requirements for teaching grammar and punctuation in the National Curriculum for English (DfE, 2014).

Why did I write this book?

First and foremost, I am someone who has a fascination with English grammar – in fact, I love it. This makes me curious about the way the English language is structured and how it works. I want children to share this fascination and curiosity, but, too often, I hear teachers say that their pupils find grammar boring. I don't want this to be the case, so one of my aims in writing this book is to help teachers find ways of making grammar and punctuation interesting and enjoyable, thus encouraging an interest in the children they teach. If teachers enjoy teaching grammar and punctuation skills, children are more likely to enjoy learning them.

Often, when I run grammar and punctuation training courses, teachers express concerns about their own subject knowledge. The updated National Curriculum, introduced in 2013 (DfE, 2014), significantly raises expectations in terms of the grammar and punctuation that must be taught by the end of KS2. This has taken many teachers by surprise and has caused a great deal of consternation: primary teachers have never had to teach grammar in this depth before and, in many cases, they have never been taught it in such detail themselves when they were at school. There are some fortunate ones who have been taught grammar, albeit in a formal way, and those who have gained a good understanding of grammar through learning a foreign language. However, this previously gained knowledge may not necessarily help because much of the terminology has changed and there are some grammatical features that appear to be missing from the curriculum. For example, where are the connectives? Where are the gerunds? And what about interjections?

For teachers who were never taught grammar in an explicit manner, there are many questions. For example, what is meant by a perfect tense and what on earth is this thing called the subjunctive? There is also the tricky problem with punctuation. How are teachers supposed to teach hyphens and semi-colons when many children are still struggling to put their full stops and commas in the correct places?

This would not necessarily be a problem if the National Curriculum (DfE, 2014) provided the guidance needed to teach the statutory requirements, but it has not done so. It appears that teachers are expected to work it out by themselves and although there is a glossary which is intended to help, it does not. So much of the guidance is vague and does not define the key knowledge that children need in order to master the grammatical skills and punctuation required by the end of Key Stage 2.

Therefore, a second aim of this book is to help provide the essential knowledge that is missing from the National Curriculum (DfE, 2014). Each statutory requirement is explained and set in context related to what should have already been taught and what is yet to come. Success in teaching grammar will come from the secure knowledge that children have been taught well in previous years, meaning that each year group teacher can concentrate on what he or she must teach his or her specific year group.

The National Curriculum (DfE, 2014) is based on a strong sense of progression which specifies the part each year group must play. Interestingly, no year group has too much to cover: in Lower Key Stage 2, there are only six grammar and three punctuation statutory requirements which can be introduced, developed and consolidated over the two years. In Upper Key Stage 2, there are seven grammar and six punctuation statutory requirements also to be worked on over two years. Therefore, the teaching of this new knowledge should not be onerous provided that the children are not having to play catch-up with previous learning.

The book has four parts which follow a logical sequence.

Part 1

Part 1 recaps on the basics. When talking about the basics, I am referring to the Key Stage 1 statutory requirements as well as other essential knowledge, which is more implicit than explicit within the National Curriculum. We cannot ignore the basics, although teachers should work on the premise that these skills have been well taught before children enter Key Stage 2.

It would be useful for Year 3 teachers to spend just a couple of weeks at the start of the year checking what has been taught and understood in order to identify any gaps. However, if there are gaps, these should be addressed and closed rapidly before embarking on the Years 3 and 4 statutory requirements. Once any gaps have been closed, though, they should not be ignored. They need to be revisited on a regular basis in order to prevent children forgetting them.

The basics are divided up into three categories: *word, sentence* and *text*. For each of these, key knowledge is discussed and aligned with the year groups in which each is taught. There are also some starting points for revisiting and consolidating understanding.

Parts 2 and 3

Parts 2 and 3 unpick and explain each Key Stage 2 statutory requirement. Each statutory requirement is contained within its own subsection, which follows the same format.

Essential knowledge

In this subsection, the essential knowledge and skills that children need to master the statutory requirement is explained. Examples are provided and links are made with previous learning and learning that is yet to come. This is here to help raise teachers' self-confidence in their own subject knowledge. It is essential to read and digest all the information before embarking on any of the teaching activities.

Introductory teaching

Often, the hardest part of teaching grammar is introducing a new concept for the first time. Each statutory requirement for grammar has been given its own suggested introductory sequence, which should ideally be covered in a session that lasts between 20 and 30 minutes. This is only an introduction, though, and will obviously need to be followed up on subsequent days.

I believe that if you try to teach grammar, particularly when introducing new learning, for more than 30 minutes at a time, it can start to have a detrimental effect on the children. If something feels complicated and the children are obviously finding it difficult, it is preferable to break the learning down into manageable chunks.

By working in shorter focused sessions, there are more opportunities for recapping at the start of each new session. I have come across schools where grammar is only taught for a one-hour session each week and then is not taught again until the following week. That makes it so much harder for the children to retain the learning and the likelihood is that teachers will spend more time reteaching instead of recapping.

Therefore, each statutory requirement has its own suggested introductory sequence. They are only suggestions, though, which are there to be adapted or completely changed if desired.

Little and Often activities

Little and Often activities are exactly as they sound: short activities that last no longer than about 5 minutes but take place on a regular basis – ideally, every day. They could be part of the literacy lesson but could equally be planned for any time within the school day. They could be useful 'early morning work' tasks or provide a thought-provoking 5 minutes before the children get ready for lunch or before they head home at the end of the day. Their purpose is to provide opportunities to revisit all current and previous learning.

Once a new concept has been introduced, it is essential that it is revisited many times across the key stage so that the children remember, practise and deepen their understanding.

Obviously, after a statutory requirement has been introduced for the first time, it is hugely important that there are many opportunities for the children to practise and consolidate the learning. However, teachers also need to keep an eye on all previous learning: statutory requirements that have been taught in the academic year, but also all of those from previous ones.

Each statutory requirement has some suggested Little and Often activities, but these are only suggestions. I hope teachers will use some activities and then be inspired to create similar ones themselves.

Finding examples in reading

If children are to understand and use the features of grammar and punctuation they are learning about, they need to see them in action, and this is where reading is important.

However, there is a word of caution here. In my opinion, the prime reason for reading is either for enjoyment or for finding information. The National Curriculum states that all children should *develop the habit of reading widely and often, both for pleasure and information* (DfE, 2014). Considering this, we should think carefully about how we alert children to grammatical structures and punctuation in their reading, as the last thing we would want is to kill the pleasure of reading by doing so.

Therefore, when reading a class novel to the children, never stop to point out the grammar or punctuation – save it for later. It is far better to return to a good example the day after and tell the children that you noticed something interesting when you were reading the book to them. At that point, share the specific example with them, either by using a visualiser or reading aloud. Link the example to the statutory requirement that it relates to in order to consolidate the learning.

Applying in writing

You only ever really know whether something has been understood when it starts to be used. Therefore, as we do not want children to only see their grammar learning in isolation, it is crucial to encourage them to use their new knowledge in their own speech and writing. It is for this reason that each subsection contains an Applying in Writing section.

For some of these, there is a specific writing activity that is suitable for trying out the skill that has just been taught, whereas for others there is a reminder to try to use the particular aspect of grammar or punctuation in a piece of writing without detracting from the overall coherence.

Terminology

Each subsection ends by listing all the terminology that pertains to the statutory requirement. This includes both terminology from the specific year group, as listed in Appendix 2 of the National Curriculum for English, as well as specific terminology that has already been learnt in previous years.

Knowing and using the correct terminology is an important aspect of learning grammar. If children don't know the correct terms, it is harder for them to talk about what they have learnt. There is also the expectation that children will be confident with the grammar and punctuation terminology when they sit the end of Key Stage 2 test as it will not be explained at the time.

Ideally, there will be a whole-school commitment to using the terminology, as identified in the National Curriculum, correctly and consistently.

Part 4

This part is entitled 'You've taught it but have they learnt it?' for a reason that, as so often, we may think that we have taught something and are therefore in a position to move on, when in fact nothing has really been learnt. That is why it is necessary to keep checking what children have learnt and to adjust our teaching in the light of what we find out.

Part 4 is not about testing, but about providing frequent short tasks that can assess what the children have learnt and can indicate next steps in teaching.

The tasks are either based on reading or writing, although there is also a benefit in giving children experience of different types of questions which may be asked in a test.

There are also some thoughts about strategies to support children who need to catch up.

At the end of the book you will also find a glossary of all the terms used and, finally, in the References section, a list of all the books that have been referred to in the Finding Examples in Reading sections.

Planning for progression

When the National Curriculum was rewritten and introduced in 2013, rather than working to levels, each year was told what was expected of it. Inevitably, it has taken a few years for this to work its way through. However, hopefully, we have now arrived at a point where each year group is playing its part and teaching the content which it has been allocated. It is not an easy thing to do, as reading and writing are not built on chronological skills, and there will be occasions where there is a temptation to teach things out of sequence.

However, if all year groups can keep to the sequence and focus on the part of the curriculum that is theirs to teach, there is a good chance that all the statutory requirements can be taught well and children will leave Key Stage 2 with a confident understanding of the grammar curriculum.

So how do we ensure that this happens? First, teachers must have a secure subject knowledge of what they need to teach, and I am hopeful that this book will help to achieve this.

Teachers also need to be confident that the content allocated to earlier years has been taught well and revisited so that there is a firm foundation on which to build. Therefore, teachers not only need to know the National Curriculum content that relates to the year group that they teach, but a wider knowledge of the entire National Curriculum.

There are also decisions to be made about what, how and when to teach the statutory requirements. In order to gain the best and longer lasting learning, I believe that the teaching of grammar should be at the heart of the entire curriculum and not restricted to grammar sessions.

Of course, there should be a dedicated grammar session at some point during each week, but no longer than half an hour at a time. In order to ensure that the learning in these sessions becomes embedded, there should be many opportunities to consolidate the learning throughout the week, meaning that when the next dedicated grammar session occurs, it does not feel that the learning is starting all over again.

There should be some links to the grammar focus, through spoken language, reading or writing, in every literacy lesson, as well as the Little and Often activities described earlier. In addition, every possible opportunity should be taken to apply the grammar and knowledge across the curriculum. One implication here is that children are required to write for a range of purposes across the curriculum rather than just filling in facts on a worksheet.

You will also notice that there is no mention of worksheets and no photocopiable material is contained within the book. This is because generally worksheets are not needed and can have a detrimental impact on learning by closing down the children's thinking. This is particularly the case when a child is faced with a worksheet that asks them just to fill in the blank spaces.

I believe that learning is far more productive when it is based on talk and when children have the opportunity to make choices. If that is aligned with a teacher's good subject knowledge, the learning has more meaning and starts to become memorable.

Think about how to plan for multiple coverages of the statutory requirements over a two-year period – either Years 3 and 4 or Years 5 and 6.

Decide where each statutory requirement is to be introduced for the first time (Appendix 2 in the National Curriculum should provide further guidance for this) and when it will be revisited in subsequent terms. For example, for Years 3 and 4:

Using the present perfect form of verbs in contrast to the past tense	
Year 3, Term 1:	Revise tenses from Key Stage 1 (1 week)
Year 3, Term 2	Revise the progressive form from Key Stage 1 (1 week)
Year 3, Term 3	Introduce and practise the present perfect form of verbs (2 weeks)
Year 3, Term 4	Practise the present perfect form of verbs (1 week)
Year 3, Term 5	
Year 3, Term 6	Revisit past and present tenses including the present perfect (1 week)
Year 4, Term 1	
Year 4, Term 2	Revisit past and present tenses including the present perfect and the progressive (2 weeks)
Year 4, Term 3	
Year 4, Term 4	Revisit past and present tenses including the present perfect and the progressive (1 week)
Year 4, Term 5	
Year 4, Term 6	Revisit and practise the present perfect in contrast to the past tense to prepare for working on the perfect form of verbs to mark relationships of time and cause in Year 5 (2 weeks)

It will be necessary to plan out each of the grammar and punctuation statutory requirements in the same way to ensure that there is good coverage and plentiful opportunities for revisiting and deepening understanding. There is a suggested framework for covering all the statutory requirements at the beginning of both Parts 2 and 3.

With a systematic whole-school approach, the grammar curriculum is achievable and learning about it can be – and should be – fun.

Reference

Department for Education (DfE) (2014) *National curriculum in England: framework for key stages 1 to 4*. London: Department for Education.

PART 1

THE BASICS: BUILDING ON KS1 AND EYFS

Although this book mainly focuses on the Key Stage 2 statutory requirements, it is important not to ignore the 'basics', much of which should have been covered in Key Stage 1 and some of which was introduced in the Early Years. Particularly, it is useful to note how much of the KS1 curriculum contributes to children working towards or meeting the standard in writing in the Teacher Assessment Framework for the end of KS2. It is also interesting to note that roughly one-third of the questions in the yearly KS2 English Grammar, Punctuation and Spelling test are based on KS1 National Curriculum content.

The challenge is to keep revisiting earlier learning while introducing the new statutory requirements in KS2. It is worth thinking about this under the headings that appear in Appendix 2 of the National Curriculum: *Word*, *Sentence*, *Text* and *Punctuation*. This part of the book will explore these in turn. The first chapter explores words, the second sentences, texts and punctuation.

CHAPTER 1.1

WORDS

Words

All the words that are used in sentences belong to any of the eight different word classes, many of which are introduced in KS1. These word classes are:

- nouns
- verbs
- adjectives
- adverbs
- conjunctions
- prepositions
- pronouns
- determiners.

Let's spend a little time thinking about each of these in turn – about what should have been covered in KS1 and how this relates to the KS2 statutory requirements.

Nouns

This is the largest word class, as so many different words can be used as nouns. The most important thing to understand about any word class is its function: the function of a noun is to name things. There are different types of nouns, although that name applies to different types of things.

Common nouns are words that name general items rather than specific ones. They are everywhere and we use these words all the time without even thinking about them. If you look around, you will see countless examples of common nouns: *chairs, tables, books, pens, mugs, walls, carpets, windows, doors,* and so on. Unsurprisingly, it is this word class that children generally start to use first when learning to speak.

These common nouns can either be classified as countable or non-countable.

Countable nouns are like the ones listed above and, fairly obviously, they can be counted. You may have one book or two, or 20 or even hundreds or thousands of them. These countable nouns can be either singular or plural, which has implications for learning a variety of spelling rules. By contrast, non-countable nouns cannot be counted in the same way. Some examples of non-countable nouns are *stuff, money, water, sugar,* etc.

Although the National Curriculum (DfE, 2014) does not actually state when common nouns should be introduced, children will be using them constantly in their speech and their writing from a very early age. The term 'noun' is introduced in Year 2.

Proper nouns are the words that name specific people and places as well as days of the week and months of the year. Children should be taught that these specific people, places, days and months should be written using capital letters at the beginning of each word. This is introduced in Year 1, although there is no suggestion that the term 'proper noun' is introduced at this time.

The name of a person or a place can sometimes be a difficult thing to work out. The names of people are perhaps not so difficult when writing a first and second name. However, it is more complicated when writing about Mum or Dad, or an auntie or uncle.

I have just written Mum and Dad using capital letters because I have used them as names. However, the moment I start talking about your dad or Serena's mum, they are no longer specific names and therefore are relegated to common nouns, which means that they do not require capital letters. It's the same with aunts and uncles: Uncle Steve and Auntie Shirley are specific names and need capital letters, whereas *my* aunt and *her* uncle do not.

It gets even more complicated when we start thinking about places. The reason for this is that many place names contain multiple words. It's generally straightforward when we think of a country or a city, such as France or Paris, as these are single words. However, when we start naming schools or parks, for example, it becomes more difficult. The first school I taught at was Chapel End Junior School; its name consists of four words and each word requires its own capital letter. Nearby was Lloyd Park. This only requires two capital letters, but many parks have much longer names with many more words. What is perhaps more confusing, though, is that we often talk about going to school or going to the park. On these occasions, we are not providing the specific names, which means that they become common nouns that do not need capital letters.

In order that children capitalise proper nouns correctly, it is essential to ensure that they can recognise the specific names of people and places.

There are also **collective nouns**, which are words that refer to groups – for example, *team, flock, herd, congregation, troop.*

The final type of noun is the **abstract noun**, which refers to an intangible concept such as an emotion, a theme, an idea or a quality. An abstract noun does not refer to a physical object. Examples of abstract nouns are *enjoyment, carelessness, chaos, danger, solitude.*

Neither collective nor abstract nouns are referred to explicitly within the National Curriculum (DfE, 2014). However, it is interesting to note that they are implicit within the spelling curriculum for Year 2, with the expectation that many children will be able to spell words with the following suffixes: -*ness* and -*ment*. It is difficult to think of many words that end with these suffixes that are not abstract nouns.

LITTLE AND OFTEN ACTIVITY

Ensure that the children understand the difference between all these nouns. A fun activity is to ask the children to think of different actions to express each type of noun. It is best if the ideas come from the children; however, if they cannot think of any, you could suggest crouching down low for a common noun and standing up tall and straight for a proper noun. The children could form pairs or trios to demonstrate collective nouns and they could make large swirling movements to show that a noun is abstract.

Provide a list of nouns for the children to listen to and to decide which action they need to make. It is useful to think of some nouns that could fit more than one category, as this will create discussion. You may need to put the noun in a sentence so that the children can check whether they have made the correct decision and to illustrate the fact that words only ever belong to a class or a category when they are used in context.

Below is a list of nouns that could be used for this activity.

horse	*example*
pride	*song*
Peter Pan	*Cardiff*
table	*Prince Charming*
litter	*lion*
chaos	*bath*
congregation	*danger*
Rose	*team*

Pride, litter, Rose and *bath* could all, when heard, belong to more than one category.

Nouns are also at the heart of expanded noun phrases, which are first introduced in Year 2 and then revisited in Years 5 and 6, and explored in Part 3 of this book.

Verbs

Verbs are essential because every sentence and every clause needs one. Traditionally, verbs were referred to as 'doing words', but this can actually be quite misleading as verbs are much more than that. One of the reasons for saying this is that the most common verb is 'to be' and there really isn't that much 'doing' going on with it. In addition, there are many verbs that represent states or feelings rather than actions. Therefore, it is preferable to refer to verbs as the 'words that tell you what is happening in a sentence'.

There are also different types of verbs: *lexical, auxiliary* and *modal.*

Lexical verbs provide information, so they are the ones that have most meaning attached to them. If we say that someone is sneezing or dancing, it is possible to conjure up a picture of what that person is doing.

Auxiliary verbs do not provide information; instead, they provide grammatical structure and help to express tense and the form of the verb. These include the verbs 'to be' and 'to have'.

Modal verbs are used to express possibility, probability or necessity. There are only a few of these and they are explored in Part 3.

Verbs take different forms: simple, progressive, perfect and perfect progressive. All of these can be expressed as past, present or future tense verbs.

	Past	Present	Future
Simple	I slept	I sleep	I will sleep
Progressive	I was sleeping	I am sleeping	I will be sleeping
Perfect	I had slept	I have slept	I will have slept
Perfect progressive	I have been sleeping	I will be sleeping	I will have been sleeping

The present and past tense, including the progressive form, is introduced in Year 2, although children in Year 1 and Early Years will be using these in order to write in accurate sentences. Children will also have explored spelling rules for adding -s, -es, -ed and -ing when forming past and present tense, including the progressive form.

In Years 3 and 4, children will be introduced to the present perfect form of verbs to contrast with the past tense; this is explored in Part 2. In Years 5 and 6, the full range of perfect tenses should be covered, as discussed in Part 3.

Imperative verbs should be explored when looking at different sentence types, including commands, in Year 2.

LITTLE AND OFTEN ACTIVITY

Write some sentences on the board. Ask the children to tell you whether the sentences are written in the past or present tense, and whether it is the simple or the progressive. As they move through Key Stage 2, you can also include examples of the present perfect (Years 3 and 4) and the full range of perfect tenses (Years 5 and 6).

- *Harry Potter attends Hogwarts School of Magic.*
- *Class 6 is visiting the British Museum this term.*
- *The boys crept silently through the Forbidden Forest.*
- *Tom was doing his homework when his friend called.*
- *Mum and Dad were repainting the house for at least a month.*
- *While the cat was sleeping, the mice stole all its food.*
- *We are having dinner right now.*
- *We ate breakfast a while ago.*

Having identified the correct tense and form, challenge the children to rewrite the sentences using different tenses and forms. What do they have to change in the sentence? Do the new sentences always make sense?

Verbs are also visited in Years 5 and 6 when looking at active and passive, and the subjunctive form (see Part 3).

Adjectives

Adjectives are commonly referred to as describing words, which they generally are, but it's their relationship with nouns that is most important. Perhaps a better definition of adjectives is to say that they are the words that provide more information about nouns.

We often talk about adjectives modifying nouns, which means that they make them more specific.

There is no place in the National Curriculum (DFE, 2014) that states that children are taught about adjectives; however, in Year 2, they are taught about expanded noun phrases. Not all expanded noun phrases contain adjectives, but many do.

As well as being part of expanded noun phrases, adjectives are often used with the verb 'to be' – for example, *I am tired*; *that dog is enormous*.

One of the biggest problems with adjectives is that they aren't used sparingly enough. Children should be encouraged to reflect on their use of adjectives and to consider whether they need to use an adjective; sometimes a stronger noun is more powerful – for example, rather than saying 'the large, spotty dog', just call it a Dalmatian.

LITTLE AND OFTEN ACTIVITY

CREATING COHESION BETWEEN ADJECTIVES

Provide a sentence where two adjectives have been left out. The challenge is for the children to choose two adjectives to describe two different things that will work together to create a specific feeling or atmosphere – for example:

The _____ boy ran across the _____ road.

Tell the children that they need to choose two adjectives – one relating to the boy and the other to the road – that will create a feeling of danger.

The boy could possibly be described as *reckless, injured* or *impetuous* among other things, whereas the road may be *busy, icy, dark* or *winding*. It's up to the children to think of ideas that go together well and begin to tell a story. You could also ask the children to think about strengthening the verb too.

As well as creating a sense of danger, children could be asked to choose adjectives to show that something exciting, funny or strange is going to happen. For each challenge, they will need to think of different adjectives and choose them with care, making sure that they work well together.

Evaluating adjectives

Provide a short passage that has too many adjectives that have not been used well. Ask the children whether all are needed and what they contribute to the overall effect. Can they redraft the piece, cutting down on the adjectives, sometimes replacing them for better ones or by thinking of more precise nouns that remove any need for an adjective? For example:

The tired, weary, exhausted girl ran along the dim, dark road. She could hear strange, weird, eerie sounds all around coming from the green bushes. She looked ahead and saw a bright light thatched house that looked nice, warm, pleasant and friendly. She decided to knock on the brown wooden door . . .

Hopefully, the children will work out that there are too many adjectives often saying the same thing. They will need to select the most appropriate adjective each time or think of a better one. When thinking about green bushes, why bother mentioning that they are green, as that is surely the colour of most bushes? Adjectives should add value and if they do not, they should not be used.

Adverbs

Adverbs are the words that modify verbs and, occasionally, adjectives. They are sometimes mistakenly thought of as only -ly words, but there are many more words that do not end with -ly that are adverbs, and also many words that end with -ly that are not.

Adverbs provide different types of information about verbs: *when, where, how and how often something happens*. Adverbs are generally single words, but they work in the same way as adverbial phrases. Adverbs are first introduced as terminology in Year 2, although there is no statutory requirement that addresses them. Fronted adverbials are introduced in Year 4 (Chapter 2.6) and adverbs that indicate degrees of possibility are addressed in Year 5 (Part 3). Apart from that, adverbs do not receive much mention in the National Curriculum (DfE, 2014) which is surprising as they are a very useful word class.

One of the most useful things about adverbs is that they can move in a sentence. They can be placed either at the beginning or the end, and sometimes somewhere in the middle depending on what you want to emphasise – for example:

- ***Carefully***, *the waiter carried the tray of overflowing drinks across to the table.*
- *The waiter carried the tray of overflowing drinks **carefully** across to the table.*
- *The waiter carried the tray of overflowing drinks across to the table **carefully**.*

The adverb *carefully* is placed in three different positions and each time the emphasis of the sentence changes.

LITTLE AND OFTEN ACTIVITY

Provide the children with some sentences and a selection of adverbs. Ask the children to select an adverb and decide where to place it in the sentence. They must then explain their decisions.

The following are possible sentences and adverbs.

The fox stalked around the dark forest.	swiftly	contentedly
The giraffe munched the leaves at the top of the tree.	stealthily	shyly
The elephant rolled around in the mud.	mischievously	warily
The kingfisher dived into the deep water.	greedily	lazily
The fish swam in the calm ocean.	gracefully	powerfully
The monkey swung from tree to tree.	dramatically	nervously
The kitten chased the ball of wool.	selfishly	rarely
The rabbits raced around the field.	finally	regularly

The children don't have to use these adverbs and it is always useful to ask them to think of some of their own.

The most important thing about this challenge is that the children explain their choice of adverb and provide a reason for its positioning.

Conjunctions

Conjunctions are the words that join parts of sentences together: *words, phrases* and *clauses*. They can either be co-ordinating or subordinating. Co-ordinating conjunctions make both parts equal – for example:

- *bread and butter*
- *I like cabbage but I don't like onions.*

There are only seven co-ordinating conjunctions and, when placed in a certain order, their initial letters spell the word FANBOYS:

For

And

Nor

But

Or

Yet

So

The most common co-ordinating conjunction is *and*, which is introduced in Year 1. The conjunctions *but* and *or* are introduced in Year 2. The other four conjunctions are used far less frequently and don't receive any particular mention in the National Curriculum (DfE, 2014).

Also, in Year 2, children are introduced to some subordinating conjunctions: *because, when, if* and *that*.

Subordinating conjunctions are used to join clauses, but they do not join them equally; they are one way of creating main and subordinate clauses (see *Sentences* below).

There are many more subordinating conjunctions than co-ordinating ones; however, the most common ones are:

although	*as*
because	*when*
after	*wherever*
before	*whenever*
once	*while*
since	*unless*
until	*if*

Conjunctions don't hold much meaning by themselves, but they are extremely useful structural words that can show cause, time frames, contrasts and possibilities. Subordinating conjunctions show relationships between main and subordinate clauses.

Conjunctions are further worked on in Years 3 and 4 (see Part 2).

LITTLE AND OFTEN ACTIVITY

Provide two clauses and ask the children to see how many ways they can be joined with a variety of subordinating conjunctions. Once they have completed the task, ask the children to decide which ones make sense (not all of them will) and discuss the

(Continued)

(Continued)

difference in meaning. Remind them that the conjunctions can either go between the two clauses or at the start of the first clause. If it is placed here, though, they must remember to put a comma at the end of the first clause. Possible clauses to join are:

- *it rained*
- *Dave felt happy*
- *it stopped snowing*
- *I wore a coat*
- *he was going to see a movie*
- *we played indoors*

Prepositions

Prepositions are often used to describe locations or directions, but they can also be used to express time and cause (see Chapter 2.5).

They form the start of prepositional phrases that can either be used as adverbial phrases or to form part of an expanded noun phrase.

Finding examples in reading

There are several books where the entire story is based on a series of prepositional phrases. Probably the most well-known one is *We're Going on a Bear Hunt* by Michael Rosen and illustrated by Helen Oxenbury. Very young children often enjoy acting out this story and, by doing so, they learn about prepositions. Ask the children to collect all the different prepositional phrases. They could also think about their own bear hunt story, but instead of hunting for a bear to choose a different creature. They could use the same prepositional phrases or devise some of their own.

Another story that uses many prepositional phrases is *Rumbelow's Dance,* which is written by John Yeomans and illustrated by Quentin Blake. This is a cumulative story in which Rumbelow, the central character, keeps meeting new people on his journey. As each new person joins him, they carry on going and, as they do, there is a new prepositional phrase to describe the phase of the journey.

> *'It's going to be a hot day, Rumbelow,' his mother said, and she saw him off. 'I'm afraid it will be a tiring walk. Now, you know the way, don't you?'*

> *'**Along** the lane, **through** the meadow, **over** the stile, **round** the orchard, **across** the stepping stones, **behind** the water mill, **up** the hill and **down** the alley, and **into** the market square,' said Rumbelow. And he kissed his mother goodbye and set out with a spring in his step.*

This is very useful in exploring a wide range of prepositions.

There is also a good example in *The Iron Man* by Ted Hughes. At the start of the story, Hughes describes the position of the Iron Man:

> *Taller than a house, the Iron Man stood at the top of the cliff, **on** the very brink, **in** the darkness.*

It is interesting to note how Ted Hughes has used three prepositional phrases one after the other to position the character. When children are writing themselves, encourage them to sometimes use this technique. Also, can they find examples in other books where authors have done the same thing?

Pronouns

Pronouns take the place of a noun or of an expanded noun phrase. They help to make writing more fluent and less clumsy, which aids the overall coherence.

Although there are actually eight different types of pronouns that are in use in the English language, in the National Curriculum (DfE, 2014) in Key Stages 1 and 2, there is only the need to learn about three. These are: *personal*, *possessive* and *relative* pronouns.

Personal pronouns

I	*they*
you	*me*
he	*us*
she	*her*
it	*him*
we	*them*

Possessive pronouns

my	*their*
your	*mine*
his	*ours*
her	*theirs*
its	*yours*
our	*theirs*

Relative pronouns

that	*whom*
which	*where*
who	*when*
whose	

Personal and possessive pronouns are covered in Chapter 2.4 and relative pronouns are covered in Chapter 3.7.

Although children will use personal and possessive pronouns from an early age, the National Curriculum (DfE, 2014) only explicitly refers to them in Key Stage 2, and 'pronoun' is part of the Year 4 terminology.

LITTLE AND OFTEN ACTIVITY

Provide the children with a short paragraph where no pronouns have been used. Ask them to rewrite the piece choosing the correct pronoun – for example:

(Continued)

(Continued)

Sally and Pippa went to play in Elizabeth Park. Elizabeth Park is at the end of Sally's and Pippa's road. Sally decided to play on the swings. After that, Sally went on the slide and then Sally went on the rope ladder. While Sally was playing on the swings, the slide and the rope ladder, Pippa played in the sand pit. Pippa then joined Sally on the climbing frame. Sally and Pippa had a good time. Eventually Sally and Pippa had to leave Elizabeth Park and go back to Sally and Pippa's house.

The children should realise that they cannot always replace the nouns with pronouns as that would become confusing.

Determiners

A *determiner* is a word that determines the noun: it specifies which particular noun is being spoken of. It will also go before any modifier of the noun, such as an adjective, and it can be part of an expanded noun phrase. Many determiners also belong to other word classes. Some examples of determiners are:

the	*most*
a	*no*
an	*my*
this	*his*
that	*their*
these	*one*
those	*two*
some	*twenty*
many	

The word *determiner* is introduced as part of Year 4 terminology.

LITTLE AND OFTEN ACTIVITY

There are basically four different types of determiners:

- Articles (*the – definite article, a* or *an – indefinite article – the* refers to a specific person, place or thing whereas *a* or *an* refer to general or non-specific people, places or things).
- Demonstratives (*these, those, this, that* – these tell you which ones are being referred to).
- Quantifiers (*numbers, some, many, most* – these tell you how many).
- Possessives (*his, her, its, their, my* – these tell you who or what something belongs to).

Share some sentences with the children and ask them to:

- identify the determiner;
- decide which type it is.

Some sentences will contain more than one determiner.

- **My** friend is called James.
- **The** small boy was crying because he couldn't find **his** mum.
- **Our** hen laid **seven** eggs today.
- I know **a** girl who knows **my** cousin.
- There are **many** children in **the** swimming pool today.
- **That** lady works at **the** library.
- **Those** pencils belong to Tom.

Words in context

It is important to point out that words never really belong to a word class until they are used in context. Think of the word *fast*, for example. This is quite an unusual word because it can be used as four different word classes: a noun, a verb, an adjective and an adverb. The sentences below show the word *fast* being used, in context, in these four different ways:

- Their ***fast*** lasted all day (noun).
- Muslims ***fast*** throughout the month of Ramadan (verb).
- James is a ***fast*** swimmer (adjective).
- Sophie runs ***fast*** (adverb).

LITTLE AND OFTEN ACTIVITY

Provide a word that can belong to more than one word class. Challenge the children to write different sentences that use the words in context but as different word classes. Possible words that could be used include:

- *cross* – noun, verb, adjective
- *book* – noun, verb
- *green* – noun, adjective
- *well* – noun, verb, adjective, adverb
- *long* – verb, adjective
- *slow* – verb, adjective, adverb
- *rose* – noun, verb, adjective
- *box* – noun, verb
- *ruin* – verb, noun
- *free* – verb, adjective
- *tense* – adjective, noun, verb
- *last* – adjective, adverb, noun, verb

Runaround

A different way of exploring which word classes specific words belong to is to play a game of Runaround. This game could be played in the school hall or even outside. There could be up to four different stations that the children can run to. These would be labelled: *noun, verb, adjective, adverb*.

Call out a word and ask the children to run to the word class to which they think it belongs. There should always be more than one possible answer. Once the children have made their decision and are standing at their chosen station, say the word once more, but this time also use it in a sentence. The children can either choose to stick with their original decision or change their mind, having heard the word in context and 'run around' to what they now believe is the correct word class.

Reference

Department for Education (DfE) (2014) *National curriculum in England: framework for key stages 1 to 4*. London: Department for Education.

CHAPTER **1.2**
SENTENCES, TEXTS AND PUNCTUATION

Sentences

Words by themselves do not really hold much meaning: it's only when we start to put them into sentences that they begin to make sense.

Sentences are mentioned first in Year 1 of the National Curriculum (DfE, 2014): children are expected to write sentences, sometimes joining different parts with *and*, and to begin to punctuate them with capital letters and full stops. They should also be taught to use question marks and exclamation marks if appropriate.

In Year 2, children are expected to write sentences in different forms: statements, questions, exclamations and commands. They are also expected to join clauses and phrases using co-ordinating conjunctions and some subordinating conjunctions (*if, when, because* and *that*).

The sentence knowledge increases in Key Stage 2 by extending the range of sentences with more than one clause, adding adverbial phrases which can move their position in a sentence (Chapter 3.4) and using increasingly complex structures such as subjunctive and passive forms, and relative clauses (Chapter 3.1).

The word 'sentence' is part of the Year 1 terminology.

Understanding sentences is not easy, but I have yet to find a way of explaining them better than by the use of sentence bags which were introduced by the National Literacy Strategy through the *Grammar for Writing* materials that were produced in 2000.

Sentence bags

The idea of the sentence bag is that it can be used to show visually how sentences are made up from smaller elements: *clauses, phrases* and *words*.

Sentence bags work in the same way as Russian dolls. Within the largest bag, there is a smaller bag. Within the second bag there is a third, and within that one, there is a final smaller one.

The four bags are labelled as follows:

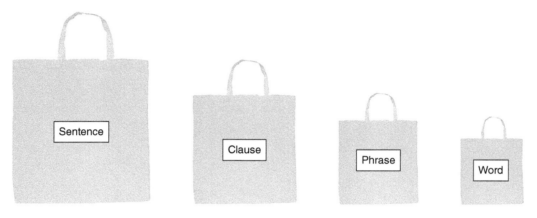

Figure 1.2

You also need some ready prepared strips of card with the following on them:

* Words: *dog*   *barked*   *big*
* Phrases: *the big dog*   *was barking*   *in the garden*
* Clauses: *when I arrived   because it was lonely   which was called Bob*

Below are the instructions for carrying out an activity using a sentence bag.

Produce the **sentence** bag, displaying label.

We teach children that a sentence is 'a group of words that go to together to make sense'. However, within that sentence, there are smaller units of sense.

Take out the **clause** bag (displaying label) from the sentence bag.

Sentences are made up of clauses.

Take out the **phrase** bag (displaying label) from the clause bag.

Clauses are made up of phrases.

Take out the **word** bag (displaying label) from the phrase bag.

Phrases are made of words. These are the smallest units of sense within the sentence.

Look at the three **words**. Get the children to identify that these are a **noun**, a **verb** and an **adjective**. It is worth making the point that for many words, you need context before knowing which word class that they belong to; however, *dog, barked* and *big* are quite straightforward.

Return the words to the word bag and put this inside the phrase bag. Take out the first phrase – *the big dog* – and display this. Make the point that words go together to form phrases and that this is a **noun phrase** – a group of words that work together in the sentence in the same way as a single noun. This is a short noun phrase, but we could make it longer – for example:

o   *the enormous great furry dog;*
o   *the small fluffy dog with the big paws;*
o   *the increasingly tired and irritable dog.*

If there are a group of words that act like the noun in the sentence (but not including a verb), we have a noun phrase.

Take out the second phrase – *was barking* – and display this.

This is known as a **verb chain** and in this case, it is a past progressive. Very often in English, we need a phrase to express the full force of the verb – a group of words that go together – for example, expressing when the verb happened:

o   *might have been barking;*
o   *could have barked;*
o   *should bark.*

These examples are helpful when talking about using modal and auxiliary verbs. It is worth using the term 'verb chain' quite early. If you ask children to look for the verb in a sentence, they are likely to look for a single word and often it will be more than one word, so you need to alert children to verb chains.

Take out the third phrase – *in the garden* – and display this. This is an interesting phrase because it changes its function depending where you place it. Make:

o   *the big dog in the garden*

Here it is telling us more about the dog, which means that it has an **adjectival** function. Like the word 'big', it has been subsumed into the **noun phrase**, giving more information about the dog.

Now make:

o   *the big dog was barking in the garden*

Now the phrase 'in the garden' is doing another job. It is telling us where the barking was happening, and this makes it **adverbial**. Also, because it is adverbial, it can move. Demonstrate this by placing 'in the garden' at the front of 'the big dog was barking', thus making it a **fronted adverbial**.

Remember, adverbs tell how, when and where, and fill you in on the background of the action.

Now, move on to **clauses** by first replacing 'in the garden' in the phrase bag. Now place the phrase bag back inside the clause bag, leaving 'the big dog was barking' on display. Point out that we have already made a clause – we have a **subject** (the big dog) and a **verb** (was barking) and these are the two aspects needed in all clauses. In simple terms, if you have a subject and a verb, you have a clause.

This brings us to the sentence, because if you put a capital letter at the start and a full stop at the end of the clause, you have a sentence. This is a **single-clause sentence**. This used to be known as a simple sentence, but that expression is not used in the National Curriculum DfE, 2014). A one-clause sentence can express a single proposition (with a greater or lesser amount of detail). However, in order to express more complex ideas consisting of more than one proposition, we need to link them together.

A multi-clause consists of:

o   one **main clause** which can make sense on its own;
o   one or more **subordinate clauses** which are linked to the main clause.

The big dog was barking makes sense on its own; therefore, it is a **main clause**. Take out: *when I arrived*. This is a clause too because it has a subject (I) and a verb (arrived). However, it doesn't make sense on its own. This is due to the inclusion of a subordinating conjunction. It needs to be linked to the main clause in order to make sense. Therefore, it is a **subordinate clause**. Show that you could place this at the end of the main clause, but then place it at the front in order to make:

o   *when I arrived the big dog was barking*

We now have two clauses linked together to show the relationship between ideas – we now have a **multi-clause sentence**. This used to be known as a complex sentence, but the National Curriculum (DfE, 2014) does not use this term either.

Now take out:

o   *because it was lonely*

Again, we have a subject (it) and a verb (was), so this is another clause. However, it also does not make sense on its own, making it a subordinate clause, so it needs to be linked to the main clause. Add this to the end to make:

o   *when I arrived the big dog was barking because it was lonely*

We now have a main clause and two subordinate clauses linked to it. Finally take out:

o   *which was called Bob*

This is also a clause. The subject – *which* – in this case is a **relative pronoun** and we have a verb chain (*was called*). Therefore, this is another clause, which is subordinate, that doesn't make sense on its own. There is only one position this clause can take and that is by splitting the main clause, thus creating an **embedded clause**. This subordinate clause is also a **relative clause** because it starts with a relative pronoun. The board should now display:

o   *when I arrived the big dog which was called Bob was barking because it was lonely*

This is getting more and more complex, so the only way to really make sense of it is to add punctuation. Ask the children what is needed and why.

o   *When I arrived, the big dog, which was called Bob, was barking because it was lonely.*

If you have a subordinate clause at the beginning of a sentence, it is usually separated by a comma in order to show where that chunk of meaning ends and the next one begins. Also, an embedded clause needs cordoning off at both ends to ensure the meaning is obvious.

And that's all we need to know about sentences.

There are other examples below to be written out on strips of card and cut up to be used in the same way, ensuring that this is an activity you can keep returning to in order to secure understanding of how sentences are formed. You can make up your own examples too.

Possible words, phrases and clauses for additional activities using the sentence bag:

Words	Phrases	Clauses
boys small playing	the small boys were playing in the park	until it was tea time although it was cold who were brothers

Words	Phrases	Clauses
shops are because	the local shops are closed in the high street	because it is Sunday although the café is open which are usually busy

Words	Phrases	Clauses
princess trapped tall	the beautiful princess was trapped in a tall tower	when she was eighteen until she was saved who was called Fiona

Words	Phrases	Clauses
teacher tired shouted	the tired teacher had shouted in the assembly hall	because he was cross as he waited for quiet who was called Mr Lee

The relative clauses are only relevant for Years 5 and 6 (see Part 3). You may want to include some examples of the present perfect tense if working with Years 3 or 4 (see Part 2).

Texts

Sentences can only provide a certain amount of meaning until they are linked together to form texts. The most effective texts are coherent and well structured, and there are various aspects of grammar that contribute to this.

Coherent texts will include:

- a logical structure;
- well-organised paragraphs;
- links between paragraphs;
- fluidity;
- conjunctions and adverbials;
- pronouns and synonyms;
- consistency in tense, person and text type.

Knowledge about texts starts in Year 1 where children are expected to sequence sentences in order to form short narratives. A narrative does not necessarily have to be a story; however, it does need to be a sequence of connected events.

By Year 2, children are expected to write cohesively by using the correct tense – either past or present – and using it consistently in their writing. In addition to this, they should be making some use of the progressive form of verbs – for example, *she is running, I was singing*.

By Year 3, children will be introduced to paragraphs so that they start to group related materials. In non-fiction writing, this could include headings, subheadings and other organisational devices. They should also start using the present perfect as a contrast to the past tense (see Chapter 2.3).

By Year 4, they will be using paragraphs to organise ideas around a theme, and also making use of pronouns to avoid repetition (see Chapter 2.4).

By the time children are in Years 5 and 6, they will be using a wider range of cohesive devices using adverbials of time, place and number, repetition of a word or phrase for effect, and making effective tense choices.

LITTLE AND OFTEN ACTIVITY

GROUPING INFORMATION FOR PARAGRAPHS

This activity would work well with most types of non-fiction writing. The example below is for non-chronological report writing:

> Provide the children with various pieces of information. Their challenge is to determine which pieces should be linked within different paragraphs. You could provide the theme of the paragraphs; however, children may prefer to decide for themselves which may result in them organising the information in different, but equally cohesive, ways.

The following information could all be included in a non-chronological report about butterflies. The possible themes for the paragraphs could be:

- *Introduction*
- *Physical attributes*
- *Habitat*
- *Diet*
- *Lifecycle*

The information to include is as follows:

Butterflies can't hear, but they can feel vibrations.	The largest threat to butterflies is loss of habitat.
Female butterflies are usually bigger and live longer than male butterflies.	Rock surfaces and bare ground are critical for butterflies – they are home to the lichen eaten by the larvae.
Adult butterflies sip nectar from flowers, juice from rotting fruit and water from puddles.	Butterflies taste with their feet.
Butterflies have four wings and six legs.	Caterpillars eat leaves.
Caterpillars hatch from eggs.	To grow into an adult, butterflies go through four stages: egg, larva, pupa and adult.
The average lifespan of a butterfly is about one month.	A caterpillar's first meal is its own eggshell.
Butterflies and moths live and breed in diverse habitats, including salt marshes, mangroves, sand dunes, lowland forest, wetlands, grasslands and mountain zones.	The world's smallest known butterfly has a wingspan of just over half an inch.

Children may also locate more facts through reading to add to this.

Once the children have allocated all the facts to the different paragraphs, they could then write their own non-chronological reports.

Finding examples in reading

Ask the children to look at different types of non-fiction books. When looking at any page, provide them with a list of things that they need to do.

- Work out the theme of each paragraph.
- Look for organisational devices – headings, subheadings, bullet points, tables, diagrams, etc.
- Identify the tense that is used and whether it is consistent.
- Look for pronouns.
- Identify linking words and phrases – conjunctions, adverbials, prepositional phrases.

They could compile a table that compares the textual devices that are used in three or four different non-fiction books. They will need to notice similarities and differences; where there are differences, try to work out why. Are the text types different? Do the devices vary depending on the audience and the purpose?

Punctuation

Part 1 only discusses the punctuation that is taught at Key Stage 1, as all other aspects of punctuation are covered in Parts 2 and 3.

The punctuation covered in Key Stage 1 is the following: *capital letters, full stops, question marks, exclamation marks, commas for lists, and apostrophes for both contractions and singular possession.*

There is no doubt that the most important punctuation is the capital letter and the full stop to demarcate sentences; these are introduced in Year 1. Unfortunately, a great many children find this basic punctuation possibly the hardest part of writing. There may be several reasons for this, but essentially it seems to stem from reading. If punctuation is intended to guide the reader in order to understand a text, then surely children must notice it in their reading, and appreciate its importance, before they can start to use it correctly in their writing. However, there is a problem with this which could well be caused by the structure of the early stage books in reading schemes.

Think of the books that children are first introduced to when they start learning to read. There is usually a big picture that covers most of the page and then just one sentence under it. Often, this sentence fits neatly on to just one line. Now here is the problem: when a child starts reading a book like this and puts so much effort into decoding the words, they know that the sentence is finished because there are no more words on the page. Therefore, there is a tendency to turn to the next page and carry on reading without paying any attention to that tiny dot at the end of the sentence. Why would you notice it when there doesn't seem to be any need to? Some children do notice the full stop and the fact that it is at the end of the line. However, this causes some confusion when writing, as these are the children who will put a full stop at the end of each line regardless of whether it is the end of a sentence.

So, what can be done about this? It is essential that children start to notice the full stop and to understand why it is there; that it is telling the reader to pause before reading the next part so that they can fully understand what they are reading. Before a child turns a page, point to a full stop and check they know what it is and its purpose. The sooner they can move to texts that have more than one sentence on a page, the better. This will mean that they must start noticing the punctuation or they will not fully understand what they are reading.

It is crucial that when children are writing, teachers should insist on capital letters and full stops being correctly used. If they are not there, give the children time to go back and put them in, but make sure they do. If they are uncertain where they should go, help them but don't allow them not to be there. When modelling writing, draw attention to this essential punctuation perhaps by underlining them.

It is only when children are secure with their capital letters and full stops that they will be able to move on to master the vast array of punctuation that they will encounter by the end of Key Stage 2.

This will include using question marks and exclamation marks, which will develop along with their growing knowledge of different sentence types. Also, make sure that children are given the opportunity to write lists so that they can show off their commas.

Probably the hardest Key Stage 1 punctuation to master is the use of the apostrophe as it has two functions: to show contractions and the singular possessive. These are both covered in Year 2.

Many children find it difficult to know where to place the apostrophe or to work out whether one is needed at all.

When using apostrophes with contractions, they need to understand that the apostrophe is used to replace a missing letter or letters and to show where they are missing. In order to do this successfully, they will need to recognise the words that are being contracted – for example, *do not* becomes *don't*.

It is useful for children to look at these as a pair so that they can identify the missing letter. They could use highlighters to visibly mark the missing letter or letters.

Perhaps more difficult is the need to use the apostrophe to show possession, particularly because there is often confusion with words that are plurals.

Each time a possessive apostrophe is used, make sure that the children are checking whether the person or object which has been given an apostrophe actually possesses something.

LITTLE AND OFTEN ACTIVITY

Provide some sentences that all include words with apostrophes. Challenge the children to work out whether the apostrophe has been placed correctly, incorrectly or should not have been used at all. Ask them to also tell you whether the apostrophe is for contraction or possession. If the sentence has been used correctly for a contraction, ask them to identify the missing letter or letters; if it has been used correctly for possession, ask them to identify the possession and who or what possesses it.

Possible sentences include:

- *Let's go to the park.*
- *Tom's brother enjoys football and rugby.*
- *The girl's went to the park after school.*
- *Don't forget to do your homework.*
- *The cat's chased the mice all over the house.*
- *Theyv'e finished all the biscuits.*
- *The ambulance's blue lights flashed as it sped to the hospital.*
- *We've finished our homework.*

If the children identify an incorrectly placed apostrophe, ask them to rewrite the sentence and put the apostrophe in the correct position.

As mentioned at the beginning of this part of the book, children should have covered most of the basics in Key Stage 1. However, over the course of time, things are forgotten, especially if they are not revisited on a regular basis. This is why the Little and Often activities are so important to keep acting as timely reminders and to ensure that these 'basics' are all in place before embarking on the more challenging aspects of the Key Stage 2 curriculum.

TERMINOLOGY

- punctuation
- sentence
- noun
- expanded noun phrase
- statement
- question
- exclamation
- command
- adjective
- adverb
- verb
- conjunction
- tense
- past tense
- present tense
- progressive
- full stop
- question mark
- exclamation mark
- capital letter
- apostrophe
- comma

Reference

Department for Education (DfE) (2014) *National curriculum in England: framework for key stages 1 to 4*. London: Department for Education.

PART 2
TEACHING GRAMMAR IN YEARS 3 AND 4

CHAPTER 2.1

A FRAMEWORK FOR TEACHING THE YEAR 3 AND 4 STATUTORY REQUIREMENTS

Vocabulary, grammar and punctuation statutory requirements

The National Curriculum (DfE, 2014) states that pupils should be taught to:

- develop their understanding of the concepts set out in English Appendix 2 by:
    - extending the range of sentences with more than one clause by using a wider range of conjunctions, including *when, if, because, although*
    - using the present perfect form of verbs in contrast to the past tense
    - choosing nouns or pronouns appropriately for clarity and cohesion and to avoid repetition
    - using conjunctions, adverbs and prepositions to express time and cause
    - using fronted adverbials
    - learning the grammar for years 3 and 4 in English Appendix 2
- indicate grammatical and other features by:
    - using commas after fronted adverbials
    - indicating possession by using the possessive apostrophe with plural nouns
    - using and punctuating direct speech
- use and understand the grammatical terminology in English Appendix 2 accurately and appropriately when discussing their reading and writing

These are the statutory requirements that must be covered throughout Years 3 and 4. In order for children to fully understand and apply these requirements, they need to be revisited many times across the two school years to embed the learning.

Part 2 will address each statutory requirement in turn, exploring what needs to be learned and suggesting a number of activities that will consolidate the learning.

Below is a suggested framework for introducing, practising and revisiting all the statutory requirements in Years 3 and 4, as well as revisiting the Key Stage 1 statutory requirements. This is only a suggested framework and there is no reason why they should not be addressed in other orders. However, by using a framework such as this, you will ensure that you are covering all the requirements on numerous occasions.

Year 3

	Introduce	Practise	Revisit
Term 1	Extending the range of sentences with more than one clause by using a wider range of conjunctions: *when, if, because, although*	Using familiar punctuation correctly: full stops, capital letters, exclamation marks, question marks	Using sentences with different forms: statement, question, exclamation, command
Term 2	Using and punctuating direct speech	Using familiar punctuation correctly: commas for lists, apostrophes for contracted forms and the possessive (singular)	Using capital letters for names of people, places, the days of the week and the personal pronoun I
Term 3	Using **conjunctions,** adverbs and prepositions to express **time and cause**	Extending the range of sentences with more than one clause by using a wider range of conjunctions: *when, if, because, although*	Using expanded noun phrases to describe and specify Word classes: adjectives, determiners
Term 4	Using conjunctions, adverbs and **prepositions** to express **time and cause**	Using and punctuating direct speech	Word classes: nouns, verbs, prepositions
Term 5	Extending the range of sentences with more than one clause by using a wider range of conjunctions: *before, after, until, once, while*	Indicating possession by using the possessive apostrophe with plural nouns	Using the present and past tenses correctly including the progressive form
Term 6	Using the present perfect form of verbs in contrast to the past tense	Choosing nouns or pronouns appropriately for clarity and cohesion and to avoid repetition	Sentence structures: words, phrase and clauses

Year 4

	Introduce	Practise	Revisit
Term 1	Using fronted adverbials Using commas after fronted adverbials	Extending the range of sentences with more than one clause by using a wider range of conjunctions: *when, if, because, although, before, after, until, once, while*	Sentence structures: words, phrase and clauses

	Introduce	Practise	Revisit
Term 2	Choosing nouns or **pronouns** appropriately for clarity and cohesion and to avoid repetition	Using fronted adverbials Using commas after fronted adverbials	Using and punctuating direct speech Word classes: pronouns
Term 3	Extending the range of sentences with more than one clause by using a wider range of conjunctions: *while, since, as, wherever, whenever, despite*	Using the present perfect form of verbs in contrast to the past tense	Sentence structures: words, phrase and clauses
Term 4	Using conjunctions, **adverbs** and prepositions to express **time and cause**	Choosing nouns or pronouns appropriately for clarity and cohesion and to avoid repetition	Using familiar punctuation correctly: commas for lists, apostrophes for contracted forms and the possessive (singular)
Term 5	Indicating possession by using the possessive apostrophe with plural nouns	Using fronted adverbials Using commas after fronted adverbials	Using expanded noun phrases to describe and specify Word classes: adjectives, determiners
Term 6	Choosing **nouns** or pronouns appropriately for clarity and cohesion and to avoid repetition	Using the present perfect form of verbs in contrast to the past tense	Using the present and past tenses correctly including the progressive form

Reference

Department for Education (2014) *National curriculum in England: framework for key stages 1 to 4.* London: Department for Education.

CHAPTER **2.2**

EXTENDING THE RANGE OF SENTENCES WITH MORE THAN ONE CLAUSE BY USING A WIDER RANGE OF CONJUNCTIONS, INCLUDING *WHEN, IF, BECAUSE, ALTHOUGH*

Essential knowledge

Children will already have been taught about conjunctions in KS1: in Year 1 they will have been taught about *and*, and in Year 2 they will have been introduced to the concepts of co-ordination and subordination through developing the use of *but, so, because, when* and *if*.

Conjunctions are structural words that, when used carefully, express connections between different ideas. It is important for children to understand how their choice of conjunction affects meaning: they cannot just swap one for another.

Children should also understand phrases and clauses in order to understand how conjunctions work (see Chapter 1.2).

The conjunctions mentioned in the statutory requirements are only examples and, considering that three of these will already have been focused on in Year 2, teaching needs to extend beyond the examples provided. A list of the most useful conjunctions to create subordination and co-ordination are provided below.

A *conjunction* is a connecting word or phrase that is used to join words, phrases or clauses.

There are two main types of conjunction:

- *Co-ordinating conjunctions* link two words, phrases or clauses together as an equal pair.
- *Subordinating conjunctions* introduce a subordinate clause.

Useful conjunctions

Co-ordinating conjunctions

and	*or*
but	*nor*
so	*for*
yet	

Subordinating conjunctions – words

because	*as*
when	*although*
if	*once*
that	*since*
while	*wherever*
while	*whenever*
before	*until*
after	*despite*
until	

Subordinating conjunctions – phrases

as soon as	*provided that*
even though	*in order that*
as long as	*as well as*
rather than	

The above conjunctions should be introduced gradually throughout Years 3 and 4. Start with the ones mentioned in the statutory requirement, bearing in mind that, with the exception of *although*, these should all be known from the Y2 curriculum.

Introductory teaching

When starting to work on this statutory requirement, it is important to establish what the children have remembered and understood from Key Stage 1.

Can they recognise conjunctions, and can they name the ones that they have previously been introduced to?

Are the children able to tell you what conjunctions are and why they are used?

Remind children that conjunctions can be found at the start of a multi-clause sentence as well as in the middle.

Display two single-clause sentences – for example:

Grandma walked to the corner shop.

She had run out of milk.

Ask the children to think of any conjunctions they could use to join the two sentences. The most likely answer is *because*, but other suggestions could be *as, after, as soon as* or *when*.

Ask the children to explain why they can use the conjunction they have suggested. The most obvious response will be that 'it makes sense'. However, if they have used *because*, the response could be that it explains why Grandma went to the shop. If *when, after* or *as soon as* has been suggested, the response could be that it provides a time line.

Write the word *although* on the board. Explain that this is another conjunction. We use *although* when something happens in spite of something else. This is not a conjunction that could be used with the two clauses above.

In talk partners, ask the children to think of a clause that starts with 'although' and can be added to:

Grandma walked to the shop.

Once they each have thought of a clause, ask them to write the full sentence on a mini whiteboard or in their books – for example:

*Grandma walked to the corner shop **although** it was over a mile away.*

*Grandma walked to the corner shop **although** she could have caught the bus.*

Discuss how *although* is being used: that it means that something happened even though there was another option. It can also be used to make something sound surprising or when you are disagreeing with something.

Ask them to tell each other what type of sentence they have written and what it contains.

Answers should include:

- a multi-clause sentence;
- a **main clause** and a **subordinate clause;**
- a **subordinating conjunction** (although);

Explain that *although* is a **subordinating conjunction**.

This process can be used at other times when introducing new conjunctions.

To consolidate, ask the children to use the following conjunctions:

when, if, because, although

to add a clause to the following sentence:

The Iron Man stumbled off the cliff.

The children should produce four different sentences. Ask them to think of the effectiveness of each one.

To recap, remind the children that conjunctions are used to connect clauses, phrases and words. They are used to show connections between ideas and they also help to make writing more coherent.

LITTLE AND OFTEN ACTIVITIES

STORYTELLING GAME

In small groups, ask the children to start telling a story. The idea is that, in turn each child will provide a clause that will end with a conjunction. The next child will need

(Continued)

(Continued)

to provide a new clause based on the conjunction that has just been heard. Having completed this first clause, the child will then give a new clause ready for the next child to complete, and so on.

The conjunction that the child hears should affect the next clause – for example:

*Child 1: Once there was a young boy who lived alone in the woods **because** . . .*
*Child 2: He had run away from his family. He often felt scared **until** . . .*
*Child 3: A small mouse decided to become his friend. From that day on, they always looked after each other **whenever** . . .*

This can be either a written or an oral activity.

MIX AND MATCH

This is a good activity to get children up and moving (either as the whole class or in groups).

Provide each child with a piece of card that will either contain a main clause or a subordinate clause. The subordinate clause could always be the same apart from a different subordinating conjunction each time. For example:

***Although** I eat breakfast*
***When** I eat breakfast*
***Before** I eat breakfast*

The main clause will always need to be different and will only fit with one or two of the subordinate clauses.

Although I eat breakfast,	I can't stop thinking about food.
When I eat breakfast,	I am always late for school.
Before I eat breakfast,	I often do my homework.
Whenever I eat breakfast,	I feel less hungry all day.
After I eat breakfast,	I still feel hungry by break time.
Until I eat breakfast,	I always have the same thing.
As I eat breakfast,	I clean my teeth.
Because I eat breakfast,	I watch television.
While I eat breakfast,	I have cereal and toast.
Wherever I eat breakfast,	I always wash my hands.
If I eat breakfast,	I concentrate better at school.

There are no right or wrong answers with these. Some main clauses will fit with more than one subordinate clause; however, there are some clauses that do not work together at all. The main aim of this activity is to discuss how the conjunctions impact on meaning.

IN OR OUT?

Children need to join the following two independent clauses with a conjunction:

The boys climbed over the gate.
There was an angry bull in the field.

Some conjunctions will imply that the boys are climbing over the gate to enter the field – for example:

*The boys climbed over the gate **even though** there was an angry bull in the field.*

However, some conjunctions will imply that the boys are attempting to leave the field – for example:

*The boys climbed over the gate **because** there was an angry bull in the field.*

As in all these activities, children need to discuss their choices. They need to explain whether the boys are heading in or out of the field and justify their response.
   Other clauses that could be linked:

Tom climbed the ladder.
Everything from the attic had been removed.

Is Tom climbing into the attic or out of it?

WALKING THE WALL

This activity is useful either as a verbal or a written exercise.
   Provide the start of a multi-clause sentence five times each with a different conjunction. Children need to decide on a second clause to complete the sentence, taking note of the conjunction provided. Each conjunction should impact on the second clause. A photograph of a wall might help to support ideas. This can easily be adapted to work with any clause.

*You can walk along the wall **because** . . .*
*You can walk along the wall **but** . . .*
*You can walk along the wall **when** . . .*
*You can walk along the wall **although** . . .*
*You can walk along the wall **before** . . .*

Think of some other clauses that can be connected to a variety of subordinate clauses through the use of a range of subordinating conjunctions – for example:

This door cannot be opened . . .
The rusty old car was abandoned . . .
The library is busy . . .

(Continued)

(Continued)

COMBINING SENTENCES

Provide a series of single-clause sentences. Encourage children to think of ways to rewrite the text using a variety of conjunctions to create some multi-clause sentences. They need to think about these carefully, remembering that the choice of conjunction affects meaning. It is also perfectly fine to keep some single-clause sentences.

> *Mrs Baxter left the shop. She had bought bread and milk. She headed down the street towards her house. She stopped to pick up a crumpled piece of paper. There was some strange writing on it.*

Display the sentences above on a whiteboard or flipchart and ask the children what they notice. They should notice that all the sentences are single-clause sentences and this makes the paragraph sound stilted and disjointed.

Challenge them to rewrite the paragraph. They need to reduce the number of sentences to two or three by selecting appropriate conjunctions that make links between the separate actions.

Children should be asked to share what they have written and to discuss their choices. Ask them to consider whether there were a range of conjunctions that could have been used. Which ones were used the most?

Finding examples in reading

It is always useful to find examples in real books. Ask the children to keep a look-out for the conjunctions that authors are using in the books they are reading. Kevin Crossley-Holland's book *Short!: A Book of Very Short Stories* is ideal for this activity as all the stories are short and self-contained. However, any book that the children are reading will provide good examples.

Look at some of the opening paragraphs in *Charlie and the Chocolate Factory* by Roald Dahl. If you show the extracts on the board, the conjunctions can be highlighted. Ask the children to find them and to discuss why they have been used.

Two conjunctions that have been used are *because* and *although*, and these have both been used twice. It is clear in the extract how *because* has been used to explain why the grandparents have been given the bed and also why everyone in the family looks forward to Sundays. *Although* is used to show that Charlie does not have enough to eat in spite of his parents giving up their food. It is also used to explain that despite having the same food on Sundays, they do all have more in the form of second helpings. It is also important to point out how, in all these examples, that conjunctions are being used to create subordinate clauses.

> *The house wasn't nearly large enough for so many people, and life was extremely uncomfortable for them all. There were only two rooms in the place altogether, and there was only one bed. The bed was given to the four old grandparents because they were so old and tired. They were so tired, they never got out of it.*

> *There wasn't even enough money to buy proper food for them all. The only meals they could afford were bread and margarine for breakfast, boiled potatoes and cabbage for lunch, and cabbage soup for supper. Sundays were a bit better. They all looked*

forward to Sundays because then, although they had exactly the same, everyone was allowed a second helping.

Charlie felt it worst of all. And although his father and mother often went without their own share of lunch or supper so that they could give it to him, it still wasn't nearly enough for a growing boy. He desperately wanted something more filling and satisfying than cabbage and cabbage soup. The one thing he longed for more than anything else was . . . CHOCOLATE.

(Roald Dahl, Charlie and the Chocolate Factory, 1964, p4)

It would be useful for the children to notice just how sparingly conjunctions are used. This is important for them to apply in their own writing: only use a conjunction where it is needed.

Applying in writing

Conjunctions, particularly to create cohesion, should be used to effect in all types of writing. As children acquire a wider knowledge of different conjunctions, they should use conjunctions more precisely and to better effect across all writing tasks.

As an editing activity, ask them to identify the conjunctions that they have used.

Ask them to consider:

- Have they used the right conjunction in the right place?
- Why did they use a conjunction?
- Are there places in their writing where they could have used a conjunction but did not?
- Were there other devices that they could have used in order to connect their ideas?

TERMINOLOGY

- conjunction
- co-ordinating conjunction
- subordinating conjunction
- word
- phrase
- clause

CHAPTER 2.3

USING THE PRESENT PERFECT FORM OF VERBS IN CONTRAST TO THE PAST TENSE

Essential knowledge

Tense will have already been introduced in Key Stage 1; in fact, in order to achieve the expected standard at the end of the Key Stage, pupils must *use the present and past tense mostly correctly and consistently*. This includes being able to use the progressive form of verbs: a statutory requirement for Year 2.

It is obviously crucial to ensure that pupils have a good understanding of the past and present tense before moving on to introduce the present perfect form.

When looking at this statutory requirement: *Using the present perfect form of verbs in contrast to the past tense*, there is quite a lot to unpick: how do you form the past perfect and why should you use it in contrast to the past tense? The National Curriculum does not provide any rationale in the Year 3/4 statutory requirements, although, when looking at the National Curriculum Glossary (DfE, 2014), there is some help:

> Perfect   *The perfect form of a verb generally calls attention to the consequences of a prior event; for example,* he has gone to lunch *implies that he is still away, in contrast with* he went to lunch. *'Had gone to lunch' takes a past time point (i.e. when we arrived) as its reference point and is another way of establishing time relations in a text.*

I don't find this particularly helpful: it needs more unpicking to teach it well for children not only to be able to use it, but also to be able to understand it. So, let's look at an example that illustrates the difference between the past tense and the present perfect:

Past tense: *I walked, he walked.*
Present perfect: *I have walked, he has walked.*

Regular past tense is formed just by adding -ed. However, to form the present perfect, the word 'have' or 'has' is inserted. As 'have' and 'has' are the present forms of the verb 'to have', it means that the verb forms are in the present.

The word 'perfect' has several different meanings: it could mean that something is as good as it can possibly be, or it could also mean that something is complete.

The verb form is 'perfect' because the action it refers to is complete.

More importantly, though, is the question of when and why the present perfect form of a verb should be used instead of the simple past tense. There are many different reasons, which can be explored throughout Years 3 and 4, but it's best to just start with one. As the National Curriculum Glossary refers to time relations, let's consider that first.

Think about the difference in these two statements:

I knew Emma for many years.
I have known Emma for many years.

In the first sentence, which is written in the past tense, the implication is that the writer no longer knows Emma; however, in the second sentence, which is written in the present perfect, the reader can infer that the writer still knows Emma.

Introductory teaching

When introducing the present perfect form of verbs, start by ensuring that the pupils are confident with tenses and know the difference between past and present tense.

Display three words: *Jamie   visit   grandparents*

On mini whiteboards, ask them to write two sentences about Jamie visiting his grandparents. The first sentence should be written in the present tense and the second should be written in the past tense:

Jamie visits his grandparents.
Jamie visited his grandparents.

Next, display two adverbial phrases: *last week   every day*
Ask the pupils to add one phrase to each sentence.

Jamie visits his grandparents every day.
Jamie visited his grandparents last week.

Ask the pupils to discuss why they chose which phrase to add to each sentence. They should be able to tell you that it is because when the past tense is used, something has already happened at a point in the past – i.e. last week – whereas, when the present tense is used, the action is occurring now. Check at this point that there are no misconceptions. If this is secure, it is a good time to introduce the present perfect. If not, keep working on more examples.

Keep the past tense sentence:

Jamie visited his grandparents last week.

However, replace the present tense sentence with:

Jamie has visited his grandparents every day.

Draw attention (or highlight) two words: *has* and *visited*.

Ask the children to tell you what tense is 'has'. They should be able to identify that this is present tense.

Next look at the word *visited*. Ask whether this is something that has happened or whether it is something that is still in progress. They should be able to tell you that this has happened and that it is a completed action. This is a good time to also remind them of the progressive form which, in this case, would be:

Jamie is visiting his grandparents.

Return the focus to the present perfect example:

Jamie has visited his grandparents every day.

Explain that this is an example of present perfect because 'has' is present tense. It refers to a completed (perfect) action. It is used to show that something has happened, but it is a recent action. In this case it does not refer to a fixed time, although we could add a time at the end of the sentence – i.e. 'this week'.

Work through some more examples with the pupils by displaying some past tense sentences that the children will need to convert to the present perfect:

Emily watched EastEnders *last week. (Emily has watched* EastEnders *today.)*
The road flooded after the heavy rain. (The road has flooded after the heavy rain.)
Grandpa fixed the broken window. (Grandpa has fixed the broken window.)

LITTLE AND OFTEN ACTIVITIES

PRESENT PERFECT OR PAST TENSE

With the children, devise an action that indicates whether a sentence is written using the present perfect or the past tense. For example, they could hold up both of their thumbs in front of them to show present perfect and they could point over their shoulders to indicate the past tense. Share each of the following sentences with the children. Ask them to use the correct action to indicate present perfect or past tense.

The elephant has walked over the mouse.
The giraffe ate the fruit from the top branches of the tree.
Lions have always lived in Africa.
Tom has eaten all the chocolate.
The headteacher closed the school.

(Continued)

(Continued)

These are just example sentences and, over time, you could come up with many more.

As a follow-on activity, ask the children to change the past tense sentences to present perfect, and change the present perfect sentences to past tense.

CONVERTING FROM PAST TENSE TO PRESENT PERFECT

Ask the children to change the following sentences from past (simple) to present perfect:

The rabbit ran in the meadow.
The rabbit ate many different vegetables.
Rabbits played in the meadows at sunset.
Rabbits slept in their burrows.

Once the children have changed the sentences from past simple to present perfect, ask them which sentences sound right?

We often need to add something to the end of the present perfect sentence – for example:

Rabbits have played in the meadows at sunset each day this week.

Challenge the children to add some information at the end of each sentence to help in making sense when using the present perfect.

NOW OR THEN?

Have the following words or phrases displayed on cards or on the board:

today   *yesterday*
this week   *last week*
this year   *last year*

Point to each of these in turn and ask the children to write a sentence on their mini whiteboards using the word or phrase. If the word is from the first column, present perfect should be used, whereas if the word is from the second column, the sentence should be written in the past.

You could model a couple of sentences first – for example:

I have started to tidy my bedroom today.
My mum asked me to tidy it yesterday.

PRESENT PERFECT IN CONTRAST TO IRREGULAR PAST TENSE WORDS

It becomes trickier when we have to work out the present perfect form of irregular past tense verbs. When the past tense forms of the verbs are regular, it remains the same when the 'have' or 'has' is inserted. However, when the past tense is irregular, the word changes. Look at these examples:

I ate (past)   *I have eaten (present perfect)*
He spoke (past)   *He has spoken (present perfect)*

Share these examples and then ask the children to work out how to change the following sentences and record them on mini whiteboards.

Irregular past to present perfect	Present perfect to irregular past
I chose six friends to come to my party.	I have ridden my bike today.
John came into the changing room.	Alex has seen his friends today.
Lizzie drew her pet cat.	The head teacher has spoken to the whole school about the Christmas concert.
We forgot to bring our packed lunches.	We have taken our cat to the vet.
They hid behind the curtain.	Mum and Dad have written to the council.

RIGHT OR WRONG?

Ask the children to work out whether the following present perfect sentences are correct or not. They could demonstrate their answer by showing thumbs up or down. Ask the children to explain why.

I have written to my friend today. (correct)
The elephant has sat on the mouse yesterday. (incorrect)
Ellie has shared her sweets last week. (incorrect)
Tom has passed all his exams. (correct)
The footballers has won every match this season. (incorrect)

These are just some examples; it would be helpful to think of more yourself.

Finding examples in reading

You don't find many examples of present perfect in stories. However, examples are much more likely to be found in non-fiction – for example, news reports, non-chronological reports and biographies.

Share this new report which is found on the bbc.newsround website: **www.bbc.co.uk/newsround/44131736**

Nine new beaches named as safe swimming spots for summer

Fancy taking a dip off the south coast of England this summer? Well now, your list of beaches to choose from has just got longer!

The Environment Agency has added nine new beaches to the list of official bathing waters, meaning there are now 422 beaches around the UK with waters that are clean enough to swim in.

Helen Wakeham, deputy director of water quality at the agency, said: "It is wonderful news that more beaches have been given bathing status in time for the start of the 2018 season.

"Water quality has improved at English beaches giving locals and tourists a better experience as well as benefiting the environment."

Ask the children to locate two examples of the present perfect:

The Environment Agency has added . . .
Water quality has improved . . .

Discuss the reasons why the present perfect has been used in both instances.

Applying in writing

Autobiographies

Asking the children to write about themselves is a good way for them to apply their knowledge of using the present perfect as well as the simple present and past tense. In order to ensure they do this, provide some questions that will help the writing. For example:

- When and where were you born? (past tense)
- Where do you live? (present tense)
- How long have you lived there? (present perfect)
- Who are your friends? (present tense)
- How long have you known them? (present perfect)

News headlines

Headlines in newspapers are often written in the present tense. The introductory paragraph that immediately follows the headline often opens with a statement written in the present perfect form. For example:

Headline	Opening statement
Chimpanzee on the run!	Officials at San Diego Zoo have reported that Charlie the chimpanzee has gone missing.
Federer beats Murray again!	Roger Federer has beaten Andy Murray in a five-set thriller at Wimbledon.
Harry and Meghan to marry!	Clarence House has announced that Prince Harry is to marry Meghan Markle in May.

Present the children with some more headlines and ask them to write the opening statement of the news article by using the present perfect form:

Warning over Dangerous Cupcakes!
Robbery in Local Pound Shop!

Man Tries to Sell Himself on Ebay!
Duck Rescued from Lake!

All the above are headlines that have been seen in local newspapers, which are a useful source for strange and intriguing stories. It is worth looking at your local paper to find some local and topical headlines to use.

TERMINOLOGY

- tense
- past
- present
- present perfect
- verb

Reference

Department for Education (DfE) (2014) *National Curriculum in England: framework for key stages 1 to 4*. London: Department for Education.

CHAPTER 2.4

CHOOSING NOUNS OR PRONOUNS APPROPRIATELY FOR CLARITY AND COHESION, AND TO AVOID REPETITION

Essential knowledge

The children will have learned about nouns in Key Stage 1. In Year 1, children will be introduced to proper nouns as they are expected to be able to use capital letters for the names of people, places and days of the week. They are also introduced to the pronoun 'I'.

In Year 2, they should be taught to use expanded noun phrases to describe or to specify. The term 'noun' is also introduced at this point.

The term 'pronoun' is not specified until Year 4 of the National Curriculum; however, children will be using pronouns from an early age.

By the end of Key Stage 2, children should know about three different types of pronoun: personal pronouns and possessive pronouns need to be secure in lower Key Stage 2 before relative pronouns are introduced in Year 5.

The National Curriculum Glossary (DfE, 2014) provides very little help in explaining nouns:

> *Pronouns are normally used like nouns, except that:*
> * *they are grammatically more specialised*
> * *it is harder to modify them*

Children need to know that pronouns are words that can take the place of nouns or the place of expanded noun phrases:

The dog *was hungry.*
The big spotty dog with floppy ears *was hungry.*

It was hungry.

'It' is used instead of both *the dog* and *the big spotty dog with floppy ears.*

This type of pronoun is a personal pronoun. Below is a full list of personal pronouns that the children should know and use.

First person:	*I*	*we*	*me*	*us*			
Second person:	*you*						
Third person:	*he*	*she*	*it*	*they*	*him*	*her*	*them*

Children also need to know about possessive pronouns.

*Joey read **his** book.*
*It's **my** umbrella that has been broken.*

Below is a full list of possessive pronouns that the children should know and use.

First person:	*my*	*mine*	*our*	*ours*	
Second person:	*your*	*yours*			
Third person:	*his*	*her*	*hers*	*its*	*their*	*theirs*

As well as knowing the list of pronouns, it is also important for children to understand why and when we use them, and to be able to apply this knowledge in their own writing.

Pronouns can be used instead of nouns or expanded noun phrases in order to make writing more coherent and to avoid repetition, which will give it more fluidity.

The other aspect of this statutory requirement is about *choosing nouns appropriately for clarity and cohesion and to avoid repetition.*

The challenge here is to try to find more than one way to refer to a person or a thing. For example, Usain Bolt could be referred to as:

Usain
Mr Bolt
The world's fastest man
The Jamaican athlete
The world record holder

These are known as *reference chains.*

Introductory teaching

Share the sentence below and ask what is wrong with it.

The lion roared as the lion chased after the lion's prey.

There is obviously too much repetition of the word 'lion', which makes the sentence awkward and clumsy.

Ask if anyone can suggest a way of improving it. The children could have a go at writing an improved version on mini whiteboards. The improved version should be either:

The lion roared as he chased after his prey.

or

The lion roared as it chased after its prey.

Ask whether anyone knows which word class has been used to replace 'lion' in both places. If they do not know, tell them that they are pronouns and that pronouns can be used instead of nouns or expanded noun phrases. Pronouns are used to make the writing clearer and to avoid using the same nouns too much.

Point out that in the new sentence, there are two different types of pronoun: personal (he/it) and possessive (his/its).

Write two headings on the board or a flipchart – Personal and Possessive – and list the pronouns in the above sentence under the correct heading.

Share a couple more examples to help the children think of some more pronouns.

Josie and I went to the park. ***Josie and I*** *played on the swings.* ***Josie and I*** *like the swings.* ***The swings*** *are fun.*
Mum and Dad went out to dinner. ***Mum and Dad*** *went to* ***Mum and Dad's*** *favourite restaurant. Mum ate the fish special.* ***The fish special*** *made* ***Mum*** *feel sick.*

Continue to list the pronouns on the board or flipchart. Can the children think of any more?

It is worth pointing out that pronouns can take the place of quite long expanded noun phrases too – for example:

Mum and Dad's favourite restaurant in London *was Pizza Express.*

The pronoun *it* would replace all the words in italics: *It* was Pizza Express.

Ask the children to have a go at replacing the nouns or noun phrases in the following sentences with pronouns:

Lucy, Joey and Sam *visited their grandparents at the weekend.*
That is ***Joe's*** *book.*
The house at the end of the road *is derelict.*

LITTLE AND OFTEN ACTIVITIES

PERSONAL OR POSSESSIVE?

Remind the children that there are two types of pronoun they have been looking at: personal and possessive. As a group, decide on different actions to demonstrate each of these. For example, they could put hands on heads for a personal pronoun and then point to themselves for possessive ones. Share a list of pronouns with the children and they need to decide quickly on an action to demonstrate their understanding of a pronoun type. It would also be useful to contextualise each one in a sentence. For example:

(Continued)

(Continued)

my   *That is **my** book. (possessive)*

you   *Are **you** going to the park? (personal)*

we/our   ***We** are going to collect **our** new car on Saturday.
             (personal/possessive)*

he/his   *Tom said that **he** was going to see **his** favourite band on Saturday.
             (personal/possessive)*

To make it more fun and fast moving, read a short passage which has a number of different pronouns in it. Each time a pronoun is heard, the children must decide on the action.

> *Charlotte and George walked down **their** road on the way to the bus stop. **They** were on **their** way to school. Charlotte always met **her** friend Lucy at the top of the road, but **she** was often late. When the bus arrived, **it** was full, so **they** all had to stand.*

Once this has been read through and the children have completed their actions, go through each one in turn and check that the children know who or what each pronoun is referring to.

ALL CHANGE

Display or hand out sheets with a text like the one below. There are no pronouns. Either alone or as a shared activity, work through the text, deciding where words and phrases could be replaced by pronouns and which ones.

> *Medhi couldn't wait to visit the sweet factory. The sweet factory was so close to Medhi's house that Medhi could smell the fantastic smells every time Medhi stepped outside Medhi's door. Medhi wanted to take all Medhi's friends with Medhi, but Medhi couldn't take all of Medhi's friends. Medhi could only choose one friend with Medhi, so Medhi chose Joe. Joe was very excited.*

Ask the children to rewrite the short text, but taking care not to put too many pronouns in. It should end up reading something like this:

> *Medhi couldn't wait to visit the sweet factory. It was so close to his house that he could smell the fantastic smells every time he stepped outside his door. He wanted to take all his friends with him, but he couldn't take all of them. He could only choose one so Medhi chose Joe. He was very excited.*

TOO MANY PRONOUNS

Remind the children that pronouns are used to help writing to be clear and to avoid repetition. However, if too many are used, writing can become very confusing, as is evident in the example below. Tell the children that this writing is about a boy called Tommy and his friend Ryan. Can they rewrite it, either as a group activity or in pairs, leaving just the right number of pronouns and ensuring that the meaning is clear?

> *Tommy knocked on his front door, but no one answered. He wondered if he was in there. He pushed it and it opened slowly. He went into it and that's when he saw him collapsed at the bottom of the stairs. He had fallen badly so he called for help.*

There is more than one way to rewrite this; however, one model is provided below.

> *Tommy knocked on **Ryan's** front door, but no one answered. He wondered if **Ryan** was in there. **Tommy** pushed **the door** and it opened slowly. He went into the hall and that's when he saw **Ryan** collapsed at the bottom of the stairs. He had fallen badly so **Tommy** called for help.*

Ask the children to compare the two so that they can see which one is easier to read and less confusing.

PRONOUNS REPLACING EXPANDED NOUN PHRASES

Provide some sentences with expanded noun phrases in them. Ask the children to replace the entire expanded noun phrase with a pronoun.

The three small boys wearing matching jumpers *waited at the school gate. (they)*
Harry's frail and elderly pet dog, Ron, *had to be taken to the vets. (it/he)*
The empty house at the end of the road *is for sale. (it)*

REFERENCE CHAINS – THE HARRY POTTER CHALLENGE

This is just an example of how you could ask the children to think about a well-known character and to think of as many ways as possible of referring to him or her. For example, Harry Potter could be referred to as:

- *Harry*
- *Young Mr Potter*
- *The boy wizard*
- *Lily and James Potter's son*
- *Ron's best friend*
- *Voldemort's enemy*

This could be a mini whiteboard challenge where children come up with as many references as they can within two minutes. They receive a point for every idea that they have, but gain two points if they think of a way of referencing the character that no one else has thought of.

This activity could be used with many different characters from well-known stories and films.

(Continued)

(Continued)

IMPROVING

Show the children the following passage about butterflies. Ask them to rate how well it is written. Can they identify the problems?

Butterflies can live up to about a year but many butterflies only live for about three months. Butterflies lay butterfly eggs and the caterpillar hatches from the butterfly's eggs. Butterflies have six legs and butterflies have four wings. Although butterflies cannot hear, butterflies can hear vibrations.

Ask the children to rewrite it in their books. They need to decide when to use a pronoun rather than using the word 'butterfly'.

Share similar badly written paragraphs for the children to improve.

Finding examples in reading

You will find many examples of pronoun use in most books. Find an extract and ask the children to identify all the pronouns. They could highlight using two different colours: one colour for personal pronouns and another for possessive pronouns. You could use this extract from *Grandpa's Great Escape* by David Walliams. This is an interesting example, as there is a good variety of personal and possessive pronouns referring to different people and things. It also demonstrates well how pronouns have been used for both clarity and cohesion:

Grandpa's military band played out in Jack's head as he pedalled as fast as he could down the street. For a toddler's trike, it was a deceptively heavy beast, especially with his mother standing on the back, her fluffy pink nightdress blowing in the wind.

As the wheels turned on his trike so did the thoughts in Jack's mind. The boy was closer to the old man than anybody; surely he could guess where his grandfather was?

Without seeing another soul on the way, the pair finally arrived at the town square. A pathetic sight greeted them.

Dad was in his pyjamas and dressing gown, hunched over the steering wheel of the family's little brown car. Even from a distance, Jack could see that the poor man couldn't take much more of this. Grandpa had gone missing from his flat seven times in the past couple of months.

(David Walliams, *Grandpa's Great Escape*, 2015, pp56–7)

Personal pronouns include *he, it, them, this*.
Possessive pronouns include *his, her*.
Once the pronouns have been highlighted, list them in a table and ask the children to work out who or what each one is referring to.

Pronoun in context	Who, what or whose?
he pedalled	Jack
as fast as *he* could	Jack

it was a deceptively heavy brute	The trike
his mother	Jack's
her fluffy pink nightdress	Jack's mother's
his trike	Jack's
surely *he* could guess	Jack
his grandfather	Jack's
a pathetic sight greeted *them*	Jack and his mother
his pyjamas	Jack's dad's
his flat	Grandfather's
couldn't take much more of *this*	Grandfather's behaviour

This extract is also useful to explore how some of the nouns aid cohesion and avoid repetition.

Draw attention to:

- *the pair*
- *the old man*

For both, ask the children to discuss who or what they are referring to.

- *The pair* is referring to Jack and his mother.
- *The old man* is referring to Jack's grandfather.

Point out how both have been used in order to avoid saying *Jack and his mother* and *Grandfather*, thus avoiding repetition.

Applying in writing

Information writing (reference chains)

As part of learning how to write non-chronological reports, ask the children to think of an animal that they want to find out about. Give them the opportunity to find out some facts and then ask them to think of at least five different ways of referring to it – for example:

A lion could be:

- *the king of the jungle*
- *a carnivore*
- *a fierce creature*
- *a big cat*
- *a wild animal*
- *a majestic beast*
- *a powerful hunter*

Once the reference chains have been decided upon, the challenge is to use them all within an information text about the animal.

TERMINOLOGY

- pronoun
- personal pronoun
- possessive pronoun
- noun
- expanded noun phrase
- cohesion

Reference

Department for Education (DfE) (2014) *National Curriculum in England: framework for key stages 1 to 4*. London: Department for Education.

CHAPTER **2.5**

USING CONJUNCTIONS, ADVERBS AND PREPOSITIONS TO EXPRESS TIME AND CAUSE

Essential knowledge

This statutory requirement has links with two other Year 3/4 ones:

- extending the range of sentences with more than one clause by using a wider range of conjunctions, including *when, if, because, although*;
- using fronted adverbials.

There are several different parts to this statutory requirement, so it is advisable not to try to do too much at one time. The learning can easily be spread over the two years. Identify set times to look at prepositions, adverbs or conjunctions and, to start with, only consider one function at a time: time or cause.

The term 'adverb' is introduced in Year 2, whereas the terms 'conjunction' and 'preposition' are part of Year 3 terminology. However, children will have been taught to use certain conjunctions in Key Stage 1 and will also have come across many different prepositions.

This section will start by focusing on prepositions.

Prepositions

The National Curriculum Glossary (DfE, 2014) has this to say about prepositions:

> *A preposition links a following noun, pronoun or noun phrase to some other word in the sentence. Prepositions often describe locations or directions, but can describe other things, such as relations of time.*

In my opinion, this is only partially helpful, so let's think about this a little more.

The word 'preposition' means 'positioned before'. Prepositions are essential for adding additional information in sentences by creating prepositional phrases. As mentioned in the National Curriculum Glossary (DfE, 2014), they are usually used to express location and direction; however, it is interesting to note that there is no statutory requirement in either Key Stage that focuses on teaching prepositions that express place. However, if you look in Appendix 2 of the National Curriculum (DfE, 2014), place is specified along with time and cause in Year 3. The prepositions listed below are used to express relationships of time. Each one is listed with an example.

Prepositions that express time	Example
on	The party is happening *on* Saturday.
in	I will be there *in* a few minutes.
at	They arrived *at* six o'clock.
since	Joe had not seen his uncle *since* last year.
for	I have known you *for* ages.
ago	It all happened a long time *ago*.
during	Alan became ill *during* the match.
until	The Christmas lights will stay lit *until* January.
by	Tom is always in bed *by* nine o'clock.
from	The shop will be open *from* half past nine.
before	Lucy did her homework *before* tea.
after	The boys always play football *after* school.

Prepositions can also be used to express cause. There are less of these, but the following are worth exploring with the children:

Prepositions that express cause	Example
due	Sam was late *due* to missing the bus.
for	The children quarrelled *for* many reasons.
from	She was exhausted *from* lack of sleep.
because of	Lara missed school *because of* a cold.

You will notice that some prepositions are also conjunctions: *since, until, because (of)*. It is also worth noting that some prepositions that are used to express time are also used to express place or cause or both.

Adverbs

Adverbs are the words or phrases that tell you how, when or where something happens: in this section the focus is mainly on the adverbs that indicate when. These will either refer to a fixed point in time or a more general timescale.

Listed below are some useful adverbs and adverbial phrases to express time.

Adverbs that express time	Example
frequently	Ryan plays football *frequently*.
occasionally	A lunar eclipse happens *occasionally*.
often	Lucy decided to visit her grandparents more *often*.
regularly	We go to the cinema *regularly*.
usually	We *usually* choose pizza for tea.
sometimes	Abi gets up early *sometimes*.
never	Charlotte *never* gets up early.

Conjunctions

Conjunctions have already been explored in this chapter. However, when revisiting them here, we will only focus on the ones that either express time or cause.

Conjunction	Example
because (cause)	Ali was late *because* he missed the bus.
as (time and cause)	Tom stopped running *as* the bus passed him. (time) Tom tiptoed downstairs *as* he didn't want to wake his parents. (cause)
when (time)	We rushed to the park *when* it stopped raining.
while (time)	Emma did her homework *while* she waited for her mum.
since (time and cause)	Khalid felt lonely ever *since* his best friend moved away. (time) Sophie guessed they were going out *since* everyone had their coats on. (cause)
until (time)	Zara stayed in bed *until* she heard everyone leave the house.
before (time)	Rachel brushed her teeth *before* she went to bed.
after (time)	Natalie relaxed *after* she had finished all her exams.

Introductory teaching

Prepositions that express time

Start by displaying some prepositions:

- *in*
- *on*

- *behind*
- *through*
- *at*
- *before.*

Ask the children to discuss, in pairs, what these words might have in common. They may be able to tell you that these words say where something is.

Explain that these words are all *prepositions* and that this is the word class that tells the position of something – either its location (place) or its position in time. They are also sometimes used to explain why something has happened (cause).

Share this sentence:

Josie visited her nan **on** *Saturday.*

Explain that this sentence includes the preposition *on*.

This is used to create a prepositional phrase (on Saturday) expressing time because it is telling the reader *when* Josie visited her nan.

Start making a list headed **Prepositions expressing time.**

Write *on* as the first word on the list.

Now change the sentence so that it reads:

Josie visited her nan **at** *half past six.*

Explain that this sentence also contains a preposition that is helping express when Josie visited her nan. Can anyone spot which word it is?

Add *at* to the list.

Change the sentence again to read:

Josie visited her nan **before** *school.*

Again, ask the children to ask where the preposition (*before*) is this time and add it to the list.

Write three more words on the board:

- *after*
- *during*
- *until*

Ask the children to work in pairs to choose one of those prepositions to change the sentence one more time:

Josie visited her nan . . .

Discuss the examples that the pupils provide, ensuring that they are always being used to express time. Add the three words to the list, explaining that these are also all prepositions that are used to express time.

For further work, either provide the children with a different single-clause sentence or ask them to think of their own one – for example:

Tom hadn't been to school.
Medhi went to France.

Ask the children to write down as many different prepositional phrases that could extend their sentence, each using a different preposition to express time.

Recap by reminding the children that the words they have been looking at are all prepositions that are used to express time.

Keep the list visible whenever you work on these types of prepositions as a reminder.

At a different time, when the children are confident with prepositions that express time, use a similar strategy to explore both conjunctions and adverbs that are used to do the same.

Prepositions that express cause

At a later point in time, once children are secure with prepositions that express time, you could use the same format to introduce prepositions that express cause.

LITTLE AND OFTEN ACTIVITIES

CREATING A PREPOSITIONAL PHRASE THAT EXPRESSES TIME

Provide the children with a number of different sentences that need completing with a prepositional phrase that expresses time. Display the prepositions that could be used:

- on
- in
- at
- since
- for
- ago
- until
- by.

The children need to choose one preposition and then complete the phrase. There may be more than one preposition that could be used; however, they need to ensure that whichever they select, it is being used to express time – for example:

Shops are often closed . . .
*Shops are often closed **on** Sundays. (correct)*
*Shops are often closed **at** the weekend. (correct)*
*Shops are often closed **in** the village. (incorrect because this is about location not time).*

There is a selection of sentences below that need finishing off with prepositional phrases to express time.

It gets cold . . .
They waited at the cinema . . .
I went to France . . .

(Continued)

(Continued)

The meeting is . . .
Joe has not seen his brother . . .
It's only ten sleeps . . .
Amina had promised to be back . . .

This could be played as a point-scoring game where individuals or groups score points for all the different prepositions that they use. Encourage the children to use a variety.

PREPOSITIONAL PHRASE OR SUBORDINATE CLAUSE?

Quite a few words can be used as both conjunctions or prepositions. Generally, conjunctions will be used to create clauses and prepositions will be used to create phrases. For a reminder about the difference between clauses and phrases, see Chapter 1.2.

Create a list of words that can be used as both prepositions and conjunctions:

- *because*
- *until*
- *after*
- *before*
- *since.*

For each word, challenge the children to write two sentences on their mini whiteboards, one using the word as a conjunction and the other using it as a preposition – for example:

*Rachel stayed awake **until** she heard her dad come home. (conjunction)*
*Rachel stayed awake **until** midnight. (preposition)*

In the first sentence, *until* is used as a subordinating conjunction that has created a subordinate clause (a clause must contain a subject and a verb – see Chapter 1.2). In the second sentence, it is used as a preposition that creates a prepositional phrase (there is no subject or verb after the preposition).

Challenge the children to do the same thing for all the words in the list.

Alternately, write the listed words on pieces of card and have these face down in a pile. Also write the words *preposition* and *conjunction* on cards and place these face down in a separate pile.

Provide a sentence and ask the children to write it on their boards – for example:

Josh ate all his chips.

Then pick up two cards: one should be a word that is on the list and the other should either be the word 'conjunction' or 'preposition'. Show both these cards to the children and challenge them to extend the sentence according to the cards they have been shown.

TIME OR CAUSE?

This could be a physical activity in the hall or the playground.
   Create three different stations or meeting points. Each will have a sign that will say:

- *Time*
- *Cause*
- *Time and cause.*

Ask the children to stand in the middle of the hall or the playground and wait until you call out a preposition. Once they have heard it, they need to decide whether it is a preposition that expresses time or cause, or both, and quickly move to the correct station. Once they have all made a decision and are standing in the appropriate place for their answer, ask one or two to then use the word in a sentence so that they can check whether they are correct. Prepositions to be used include:

- *on (time)*
- *in (time)*
- *at (time)*
- *due (cause)*
- *since (both)*
- *or (both)*
- *ago (time)*
- *during (time)*
- *until (time)*
- *by (time)*
- *because of (cause)*
- *from (both)*
- *before (time)*
- *after (time).*

This could be a point-scoring game played in teams.

ADVERB, CONJUNCTION OR PREPOSITION?

Share a number of sentences like the ones below. For each one, ask the children to decide whether time has been expressed by the use of a conjunction, a preposition or an adverb.

Joe has been feeling tired lately. (adverb)
Joe was tired after he played a long football match. (conjunction)
Joe was tired after lunch. (preposition)
Lucy felt hungry during assembly. (preposition)
Lucy always felt hungry. (adverb)
Lucy was hungry until she ate a large dinner. (conjunction)

(Continued)

(Continued)

Our shop is open from Monday to Friday. (preposition)
Our shop never opens on a Sunday. (adverb)
Our shop is open before the other shops in the precinct. (preposition)

These are just some examples, but it is easy to think of many more. You could also ask the children to devise their own sentences to test on others. They must be sure of the correct answers themselves, though.

Finding examples in reading

Prepositions that express cause

Read the opening paragraphs of *The Ice Palace* by Robert Swindells:

> *Turn your face into the east wind, and if you could see for ever you would see Ivan's land. It is a land where summer is short and pale like a celandine; winter long and cold as an icicle. Ivan does not live there now for he grew old long ago and is gone. But the people of the pine-woods remember him. They remember him all the time, but most of all they remember him in the winter because they are not afraid any more. They have no need to be afraid, because of something Ivan did when he was small.*
>
> (Robert Swindells, *The Ice Palace*, 1977, pp5–7)

There are three examples in this small extract where cause is expressed either by the use of conjunctions or prepositions.
  The three examples are:

for *he grew old long ago (preposition)*
*in the winter **because** . . . (conjunction)*
because *of something Ivan did . . . (conjunction)*

Ask the children to locate them and to determine whether the words are prepositions or conjunctions.

Prepositions that express time

This example uses *The Iron Man* by Ted Hughes (1968); however, this activity could be carried out with any book.
  Ask the children to search through the book as a scanning exercise to locate as many prepositions expressing time as they can. Some examples in this story include:

* *Just before dawn . . .*
* *Now in no time . . .*
* *At that moment . . .*
* *In a moment . . .*
* *Before the end of the summer . . .*

- *At last . . .*
- *Never before . . .*
- *On the fifth night . . .*
- *Within a few more nights . . .*
- *For a whole morning . . .*
- *At the same time . . .*
- *At this point . . .*
- *But at that very moment . . .*
- *Meanwhile . . .*

As it can be seen, a book such as this offers up many examples of prepositions expressing time. The challenge is to notice them and to remember them so that they can be used in writing. Use these to start to make a preposition (expressing time) list that can be added to over time. Lists such as these should be visible to the children while they are writing. This list from *The Iron Man* would be most useful when writing stories; however, similar phrases will be found in all non-fiction text types.

Applying in writing

Adapting phrases

Take one of the phrases that has been identified through reading – for example:

Before the end of summer . . .

Look at how this phrase can be changed in order to be used for different expressions of time.

Show some examples to the children before asking them to come up with some ideas of their own:

Before the end of spring . . .
Before the end of the day . . .
Before the birds had flown . . .
Before everyone left the room . . .

Ask the children to come up with two or three prepositional phrases themselves, all of which must start with *before*.

Excuses

Get the children to think about a situation where they may need to think of some excuses – for example:

Not doing homework
Being late for school
A messy bedroom

Ask the children to write down as many excuses as they can think of: some may be sensible ones but it is also an opportunity to have a bit of fun.

Display a list of prepositions and conjunctions that express cause:

- *because*
- *as*
- *due*
- *for*
- *from*
- *since*
- *because of.*

The children can then start to create their own list – for example:

Why I was late to school.

*I overslept **because** my mum forgot to wake me.*

*I was too tired to get out of bed **due** to lack of sleep.*

*I had to walk all the way **as** the bus did not turn up.*

That's why I was late to school!

Cross-curricular

Prepositions and conjunctions expressing time can be consolidated during mathematics units on time, particularly when working out the distance between places and how long it might take to travel.

Also, in mathematics, create Venn diagrams. Use the words that have been covered as conjunctions, adverbs and prepositions. With three overlapping circles, sort out which words belong to which word classes or whether they belong to more than one.

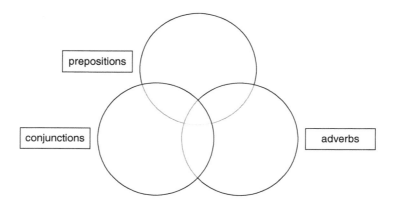

TERMINOLOGY

- preposition
- adverb
- conjunction
- phrase
- clause

Reference

Department for Education (DfE) (2014) *National curriculum in England: framework for key stages 1 to 4*. London: Department for Education.

CHAPTER 2.6

USING FRONTED ADVERBIALS AND COMMAS AFTER FRONTED ADVERBIALS

Essential knowledge

The term 'adverb' should be introduced in Year 2; however, adverbs do not receive any other mention as a specific statutory requirement in the Key Stage 1 National Curriculum, including Appendix 2. However, in order to be able to write coherently, adverbs are a crucial requirement in writing.

The National Curriculum Glossary (DfE, 2014) explains adverbs as follows:

> *The surest way to identify adverbs is by the ways they can be used: they can modify a verb, an adjective, another adverb or even a whole clause. Adverbs are sometimes said to describe manner or time. This is often true, but it doesn't help to distinguish adverbs from other word classes that can be used as adverbials, such as preposition phrases, noun phrases and subordinate clauses.*

This explanation does not really provide enough information to be able to teach them well.

The most important knowledge to acquire about adverbs is that most often they are related to verbs and they will tell us *where*, *when* or *how* something happened.

Often children are advised to look for words ending with -ly in order to identify adverbs; however, this is a bit of a red herring, particularly as most adverbs do not end in this way and there are also many words ending in -ly which are not adverbs – for example, 'silly', 'rely', 'jelly'.

If children are only looking for -ly adverbs, they will be ignoring the adverbs that tell us *when* and *where*.

This statutory requirement is not just about adverbs, though; it is also about adverbial phrases, which include prepositional phrases, and subordinate clauses. For the difference between phrases and clauses, see Chapter 1.2.

Adverbs and adverbial phrases can be placed at different points within a sentence; when they are placed at the beginning, they are called fronted adverbials. The last word of the fronted adverbial needs a comma after it in order to show that it is separate from the main part of the sentence. The comma also tells the reader to take a slight pause before reading on in order to separate the meaning.

Introductory teaching

Recap on previous knowledge first. Ask if anyone can explain what an adverb is. Adverbs are the words that tell you when, where or how something is happening. They can be single words, but they can also be phrases. Ask the children for some examples to list on the board or a flip chart.

Display the following sentence on a piece of card:

Dina chatted to her friends.

Ask the children to come up with some ideas about where Dina may have chatted to her friends – for example, *in the noisy playground*. Write this on a piece of card and place it after the original sentence. The two cards should now read:

*Dina chatted to her friends **in the noisy playground**.*

Ask the children to also come up with more ideas about how, where and when Dina chatted to her friends – for example, *excitedly, with great secrecy, during the evening, at the weekend, at the bus stop*.

Choose some of the ideas to also write on cards and place after the original sentence. Examples could be:

*Dina chatted to her friends **during the evening**.*
*Dina chatted to her friends **excitedly**.*

Remind the children that in each sentence, an adverbial phrase has been added to the main part of the sentence. These adverbial phrases tell when, where or how something is happening. In these examples, the phrases have been placed at the end of the sentence; however, the interesting thing about adverbials is that they can move. If we wanted to, we could move them to the front of the sentence. At this point, physically move the three adverbials to the front of the sentences so that they now read:

In the noisy playground *Dina chatted to her friends.*
During the evening *Dina chatted to her friends.*
Excitedly *Dina chatted to her friends.*

As the adverbials have been moved to the front of the sentence, they have become fronted adverbials. They now need some punctuation to separate the fronted adverbial from the clause; to illustrate this, either add a comma by writing one directly after each adverbial phrase or use commas written on separate pieces of card and insert them between the fronted adverbial and the clause. Explain that the comma is placed there to tell the reader to make a slight pause in order to help separate meaning.

In the noisy playground, *Dina chatted to her friends.*

During the evening, *Dina chatted to her friends.*

Excitedly, *Dina chatted to her friends.*

To consolidate this, provide a different sentence – for example:

The squirrels ran up the drainpipe.

Ask the children to write three fronted adverbials to link to this sentence, telling when, where and how the squirrels ran up the drainpipe.

It is important to point out that not every sentence needs a fronted adverbial. They are equally useful at the end of the sentence. However, if the writer chooses to use a fronted adverbial, they are quite likely wanting to emphasise the *where, when* or *how*. This helps the reader to cue into what is happening – for example, when time passes.

Recap the learning as follows:

Adverbs and adverbial phrases tell the reader when, where and how something happened. They can either go at the beginning or the end of the sentence. If they go at the beginning, they are called fronted adverbials and they need a comma directly after them in order to separate meaning.

LITTLE AND OFTEN ACTIVITIES

STARTING WITH A CONJUNCTION

It is important for children to know that conjunctions don't always come in the middle of two phrases or clauses; sometimes they come at the beginning.

ACTIVITY 1

Write one conjunction on the whiteboard – for example:

- *when*
- *although*
- *before.*

Give the children five minutes to write as many sentences as possible, starting with the chosen conjunction. They can either do this in their writing book or on a mini whiteboard. They need to ensure that the sentence is punctuated properly with a capital letter at the start, a full stop at the end and a comma to separate the clauses. This activity will also ensure that the children are writing multi-clause sentences with both a main and a subordinate clause.

ACTIVITY 2

Write a single-clause sentence on the board – for example:

It is raining.

(Continued)

(Continued)

Next, provide a number of subordinating conjunctions for the children to think about:

- *although*
- *whenever*
- *until*
- *because*
- *if.*

The challenge for the children is to place each of the conjunctions in front of the single clause and then to write the entire sentence by adding another (main) clause – for example:

Although *it is raining, we will still take the dog for a walk.*

Because *it is raining, the football match has been cancelled.*

If *it is raining, we will need to wear wellington boots.*

The key point of this activity is to explore and discuss how different conjunctions affect meaning.

LOCATION, LOCATION, LOCATION

Show the children a picture of a place. It could be of any place – for example, a tower block, a desert island, a forest, a bridge, etc.

Ask them to look at the picture and decide how they can focus on different locations within the picture. Linking with the work they will have already carried out on prepositions, ask them to create some 'where' adverbials – for example:

Beneath *the cloudy sky.*
In front of *the iron railings.*
Between *the tall imposing towers.*

Once the children have come up with as many adverbials as they can think of, ask them to select three or four to use as fronted adverbials in order to describe the setting. These could be used to create a short list poem – for example:

Beneath *the cloudy sky, Tower Bridge protects the city.*

Between *the tall imposing towers, ships sail smoothly down the Thames.*

In front of *iron railings, a small child stands and stares.*

ADDING FRONTED ADVERBIALS

Ask the children to insert a fronted adverbial before each sentence below. The adverbials can either tell the reader when, where or how. Remind the children to punctuate correctly by always inserting a comma after the fronted adverbial.

- *Trains are often late.*
- *Platforms are overcrowded.*
- *Many trains are diverted.*
- *Most trains do not have a guard on board.*
- *Passengers rush to get on board before the doors close.*
- *Passengers are angry.*

Once all sentences have been created, ask the children to evaluate the effectiveness of the fronted adverbials they have used.

As an extension, ask the children to combine the sentences to form a paragraph describing the chaos at some rail stations. They should choose to use some fronted adverbials to help create cohesion, but not all of them.

Finding examples in reading

Fronted adverbial collectors

Ask the children to have a look at news stories in newspapers that you have at school or at home. These could be either local or national newspapers. They can also look at newspapers online or go to **bbc.newsround**.

The challenge is to record as many fronted adverbials as they can find. These will either be at the start of paragraphs or may link sentences within them.

Provide a few fronted adverbials to start with and ask the children to see how many more they can find.

- *Last week,*
- *About an hour later,*
- *After that,*
- *Ten days after setting off,*
- *During the event,*

Using fronted adverbials when writing stories

Over time, ask the children to notice and record fronted adverbials in the stories they are reading. This could be carried out as a class or a group, or individually.

Initially, the fronted adverbials should be listed under three headings: beginning, middle and end depending on where they are found in the story. As the children identify more fronted adverbials, keep adding to the list so that it acts as a reference bank when the children are writing. Below is an example of a chart that has been started using fronted adverbials found in some short stories from *The Story Shop* anthology, compiled by Nikki Gamble.

Beginning	Middle	End
When King Hrothgar came to the throne of Denmark, ('The Grendel' – Anthony Horowitz).	*As ill luck would have it* ('The Dream', retold by Robert Leeson). *As soon as it was spring and the sun warmed up the ground,* ('Thumbelisa' – Hans Christian Andersen).	*From that day,* ('Tiger Story, Anansi Story' – Philip Sherlock). *And since that time,* ('How Not to be a Giant Killer' – David Henry Wilson).

Examples can also be located in reading to explore how writers make good use of fronted adverbials to explain when, where and how things happen in a story. These can also be listed under different headings. The example comes from 'The Grendel' in *Myths and Legends* by Anthony Horowitz and are listed under the headings When, Where and How:

When	Where	How
When King Hrothgar came to the throne of Denmark, *The next morning,* *Only then,*	*In the banqueting hall,* *And inside the hall,*	*Curled up in the darkness of the swamp,* *Gliding through the shadows,* *At the touch of its hands,* *Even as its claws tightened,* *Howling with pain,*

Over time, add to the list with examples from different stories. Short stories are always a useful source as there are often a good variety contained with a few pages.

It is not just about collecting large numbers of fronted adverbials, though; we want children to evaluate their effectiveness. Once a collection has been amassed, as in the example above, ask the children to discuss the ones they like the most. This should move them away from just using the more usual ones such as *once upon a time, one day, later, the next morning, finally, etc.*

Applying in writing

Fronted adverbials for focusing on setting

In the book *Vulgar the Viking and the Rock Cake Raiders*, fronted adverbials are used in an interesting way in order to focus on the setting:

> ***In a messy bedroom, in a small hut, somewhere near the sleepy town of Blubber***, *a young boy named Vulgar threw back his covers and leapt out of bed.*

(Odin Redbeard, Vulgar the Viking and the Rock Cake Raiders, 2012)

I like the way this is written because the writer uses three fronted adverbials in order to determine where the story is taking place. This is a useful technique to pick up on in writing in order to establish the location of the setting.

The idea of a story starting off in a room that is in a building near to somewhere else is quite an easy one to adapt – for example:

In a small cosy dormitory, in a magical school for wizards, somewhere near a forbidden forest, a young wizard lay snug in his bed.

When they are planning a story, ask the children to think where it is going to start. Can they create a series of fronted adverbials to establish where it is taking place and to introduce the character? To start with, they could use the same openings:

In . . .
in . . .
somewhere near . . .

Remind them that after each fronted adverbial, they will need to insert a comma in order to separate each one.

They could also try reversing the order:

Somewhere near . . .
in . . .
in . . .

Share a wider list of prepositions so that the children are not just restricted to the ones in the example.

by, next to, beside, between, over, under, on

Challenge the children to develop a setting description following on from their three fronted adverbials.

TERMINOLOGY

- adverb
- adverbial
- fronted adverbial
- preposition
- comma

Reference

Department for Education (DfE) (2014) *National curriculum in England: framework for key stages 1 to 4*. London: Department for Education.

CHAPTER 2.7
YEARS 3 AND 4 PUNCTUATION

Pupils should be taught to indicate grammatical and other features by:

- using commas after fronted adverbials;
- indicating possession by using the possessive apostrophe with plural nouns;
- using and punctuating direct speech.

Essential knowledge

Pupils should leave Key Stage 1 with a good knowledge of basic punctuation. They should have covered and be using the following correctly and consistently:

- capital letters for the start of a sentence and for the names of people, places and the days of the week;
- full stops;
- question marks;
- exclamation marks;
- commas for lists;
- apostrophes for contractions and for singular possession.

It may be worth spending the first few weeks in Year 3 going over the KS1 punctuation, but this should not take too much time before moving on to new knowledge.

Using commas after fronted adverbials

Adverbs, adverbial phrases and subordinate clauses can be placed at different points within a sentence; when they are placed at the beginning, they are called *fronted adverbials*. The last word of the fronted adverbial needs a comma after it in order to show that it is separate from the main part of the sentence. The comma also tells the reader to take a slight pause before reading on in order to separate the meaning.

Indicating possession by using the possessive apostrophe with plural nouns

Children will have learned how to use the possessive apostrophe for singular nouns in Year 2 – for example:

Josie's shoes are red.
Miss Turnbull's mood was never good on a Monday morning.

This knowledge needs to be secure before they go on to look at possessive apostrophes with plural nouns.

When it is used with plural nouns that are created by adding 's', the apostrophe goes at the end of the word after the 's' – for example:

The girls' shoes are red.

It is useful to compare this with a similar sentence where the noun is singular:

The girl's shoes are red.
The girls' shoes are red.

In the first sentence, there is only one girl who has red shoes; however, in the second sentence there are at least two girls with red shoes and possibly many more.

Using and punctuating direct speech

The most important point to make about direct speech is that it should be used sparingly and for good reason. However, if it is used for good effect, either to advance the action or to convey character, it must be punctuated correctly.

There are several conventions that govern correct speech punctuation, as demonstrated by the example below:

'What time does the play start?' asked Helena.
'About eight o'clock,' replied Dad.
'Thanks. I'll be there.'

Children need to be taught that:

- the actual words that are spoken are written inside the speech marks (or inverted commas);
- the spoken words must have some punctuation at the end: a comma, question mark or an exclamation mark if it is followed by a reporting clause (asked Helena; replied Dad);
- the speech can end with a full stop, question mark or exclamation mark if there is no reporting clause; however, this punctuation must be contained within the speech marks (inverted commas);
- if there is a reporting clause, there will be a full stop or exclamation mark at the end;
- each new line of speech starts with a capital letter;
- every time a new character speaks, it must be started on a new line.

LITTLE AND OFTEN ACTIVITIES

COMMAS AFTER FRONTED ADVERBIALS: RIGHT, WRONG OR MISSING?

Write a sentence on the board or a flipchart. The sentence may have a comma in the correct place, in the wrong place or not at all. Ask the children to look at the sentence and tell you whether the punctuation is in the right place, wrong place or missing. They could use thumbs up (for correct positioning), thumbs down (for incorrect positioning) and thumbs flat (for missing commas). Ask the children to explain their decisions, which should relate to being able to identify fronted adverbials. If the children decide that a comma is missing or in the wrong place, they should be asked where it should be placed.

Use any of the sentences below or make up your own.

- *After a while Harry decided to go home.* (missing)
- *As it was raining, all the children congregated in the hall at lunchtime.* (correct)
- *It's never easy, to say sorry.* (incorrect)
- *Whenever, Mr Thompson walked down the corridor everyone was silent.* (incorrect)
- *Ever since yesterday, evening it had rained non-stop.* (incorrect)
- *In a rush, Ahmed ate his lunch.* (correct)
- *After we watched the film we had fish and chips.* (missing)

MOVING CLAUSES AND ADDING COMMAS

Share sentences that have a main clause at the front of the sentence that is followed by a subordinate clause. Challenge the children to identify the subordinate clause. After doing so, ask them to move it to the front of the sentence, thus creating a fronted adverbial. Finally, add the comma to show where the fronted adverbial ends and the main clause begins.

- *I carried on reading after I had turned out the light.*
- *Mum sent me to the corner shop because we had run out of milk.*

(Continued)

(Continued)

- *The choir performed a recital as the crowds went about their shopping.*
- *Gran watched television after she had eaten her supper.*

SINGULAR OR PLURAL APOSTROPHES

Show the children the sentence below and demonstrate how to rewrite it so that it requires an apostrophe.

The presents that were given to Mrs Brown are under the tree.

This should be rewritten as:

Mrs Brown's presents are under the tree.

Point out that the apostrophe is before the 's' because there is only one Mrs Brown.
   Show another example, but this time it will need a possessive apostrophe for plural nouns:

The cars that belong to the teachers are in the car park.

Ask the children to help rewrite the sentence:

The teachers cars are in the car park.

Don't include the apostrophe until after the sentence is rewritten and ask the children to tell you where the apostrophe should go. Ask them to explain that it goes after the 's' because we know that there is more than one teacher.

The teachers' cars are in the car park.

Ask the children to rewrite the following sentences on their own.

The books that belong to Ali are tattered and torn.
The paper dolls that Rebecca made were beautifully decorated.
The windows on the old, derelict houses need to be replaced.

For each sentence, they need to decide where the apostrophe goes, depending whether the nouns are singular or plural.

IDENTIFYING PUNCTUATION IN SPEECH

Display a correctly punctuated speech sentence – for example:

- *'What time is the last train to Oldham?' the old man enquired.*
- *'We're going to be late if you don't hurry up!' Mrs Wright berated.*
- *'I really enjoyed that film,' Tom said as he came out of the cinema.*
- *'Good luck in your exam today,' Mum said encouragingly.*

Ask the children to find and highlight the punctuation and to explain why it is used. The first two are quite straightforward, but you will need to draw attention to the comma in the third and fourth examples and make sure that the children understand that the comma is used because the sentence does not end with the speech. If you take one sentence a day for a week, the children should start to identify similarities which will help them to recognise the rules of speech punctuation.

If the children find these quite straightforward, introduce sentences that do not always start with direct speech or ones where the words are broken up by the speaker – for example:

- *Emily shouted, 'Get down from that icy wall before you fall!'*
- *'Hurry up, Dad,' Tom urged, 'we need to collect Mum from the shops.'*

PUTTING IN THE CORRECT PUNCTUATION

Display a sentence with little or no speech punctuation. Can the children add in the correct speech punctuation? For example:

- *What time is lunch? asked Lisa ravenously.*
- *'Please can I stay up later tomorrow begged Melissa*
- *You need to hand in all your homework tomorrow stated Mr Hall firmly.*

Once each sentence has been punctuated correctly, ask the children to explain why the punctuation is correct.

You can also add to the challenge by displaying a sentence incorrectly punctuated – for example:

- *'I need to collect some sponsors' for the park run on Friday David said.*
- *'Please can you help me with my literacy homework asked Saskia I've got a test tomorrow.'*

Ask the children to indicate where the punctuation is incorrect and to explain why.

CONVERTING REPORTED SPEECH TO DIRECT SPEECH

Explain to the children that sometimes writers use the exact words that characters say: this is direct speech. At other times they may just report what has been said: this is reported or indirect speech – for example:

- *'Go and wash your hands before dinner,' said Mum.* (direct speech)
- *Mum told us to wash our hands before dinner.* (reported speech)

The children should notice that inverted commas are only used when there is direct speech.

Share some sentences that only use reported speech. Ask the children to convert these to sentences that use direct speech. They need to write them and ensure that

(Continued)

(Continued)

they are punctuated correctly. These sentences need to include the actual words that the characters would have spoken.

- *Matilda said that she always loved to read books.*
- *The policeman instructed the crowds to keep to the left.*
- *The headteacher explained that the party had been cancelled due to some pupils' irresponsible behaviour.*

PUTTING THE CORRECT PUNCTUATION IN

Have a small piece of unpunctuated speech written on the board – for example:

The porridge was too hot explained Mummy Bear so we decided to go out for a walk.

My chair was broken and my porridge was gone stated Baby Bear and there was some-one sleeping in my bed.

Ask the children to identify the actual words being said in both examples. Then ask them to help you to punctuate the speech. They may need a reminder of the punctuation rules for speech – e.g. speech marks enclose the exact words spoken; punctuation belonging to the words spoken goes inside the speech marks; other punctuation goes outside the speech marks.

This could be part of a unit of work on newspaper reports using well-known stories.

APPLYING IN WRITING – DIRECT SPEECH PUNCTUATION

Provide the children with a short script. This can be differentiated for different abilities. Point out that although we can see the actual words that the characters speak, there are no speech marks in play scripts.

Late one summer evening at the local swimming pool.

Mum: (Looking suddenly at the large clock on the wall) My goodness! Look at the time. We had better get a move on.

Tom: (sadly) Do we have to go yet?

Laura: Please Mum! Just five more minutes on the big water slide and then we will go and get changed.

Mum: (hesitantly) Oh very well then but only five minutes. I don't want to walk home in the dark!

Laura: Thanks Mum! You're the best!

Mum heads towards the changing room while the children carry on swimming.

Ask the children (in threes) to act out the script thinking about what the characters say and how. They could also put in some actions.

Then ask the children to take the script and cut it up into the different speakers. Do the same with an enlarged script or have one already up on the whiteboard.

Ask one trio to act out the first two lines and model how you would start to take the script and turn it into a narrative with direct speech – for example, you may want to add in some narrative before the direct speech:

It was a late summer evening at the swimming pool. Mum looked at the large wall clock and exclaimed, 'My goodness! Look at the time. We had better get a move on.'
Tom and Laura looked sadly at each other. 'Do we have to go yet?' wailed Tom.

Ask the children to continue transforming the script into a piece of narrative ensuring correct speech punctuation, including a new line for each speaker.

For the plenary, ask the children to suggest what might happen next. As a class, devise the next line of the story, making sure to include speech. Children all have a go on the next line on their whiteboards or in their writing books. Ask some children to share and discuss what they have done.

TERMINOLOGY

- comma
- fronted adverbial
- apostrophe
- plural
- singular
- noun
- inverted commas (speech marks)
- direct speech

PART 3
TEACHING GRAMMAR IN YEARS 5 AND 6

CHAPTER 3.1
YEARS 5 AND 6 STATUTORY REQUIREMENTS

Vocabulary, grammar and punctuation statutory requirements

Pupils should be taught to develop their understanding of the concepts set out in Appendix 2 of the National Curriculum, English (DfE, 2014) by:

- recognising vocabulary and structures that are appropriate for formal speech and writing, including subjunctive forms;
- using passive verbs to affect the presentation of information in a sentence;
- using the perfect form of verbs to mark relationships of time and cause;
- using expanded noun phrases to convey complicated information concisely;
- using modal verbs or adverbs to indicate degrees of possibility;
- using relative clauses beginning with who, which, where, when, whose, that, or using an implied (i.e. omitted) pronoun;
- learning the grammar for Years 5 and 6 in English Appendix 2.

Pupils should indicate grammatical and other features by:

- using commas to clarify meaning and avoid ambiguity in writing;
- using hyphens to avoid ambiguity;
- using brackets, dashes or commas to indicate parenthesis;

- using semi-colons, colons or dashes to mark boundaries between independent clauses;
- using a colon to introduce a list;
- punctuating bullet points consistently.

These are the statutory requirements that must be covered throughout Years 5 and 6. In order for children to fully understand and apply these requirements, they will need to be revisited many times across the two school years to embed the learning.

Part 3 will address each statutory requirement in turn, exploring what needs to be learnt and suggesting a number of activities that will consolidate the learning. It will also make links between these statutory requirements and earlier learning.

Below is a suggested framework for introducing, practising and revisiting all the statutory requirements in Years 5 and 6, as well as revisiting the Years 3 and 4 and KS1 statutory requirements. This is only a suggested framework, though, and there is no reason why they should not be addressed in other orders. However, by using a framework such as this, you will ensure that you are covering all the requirements on numerous occasions.

Year 5

	Introduce	**Practise**	**Revisit**
Term 1	Using the perfect form of verbs to mark relationships of time and cause (past perfect).		Using the present perfect form of verbs in contrast to the past tense (Y3/4). Using the present and past tenses correctly, including the progressive form (Y2).
Term 2	Using expanded noun phrases to convey complicated information concisely.	Using the perfect form of verbs to mark relationships of time and cause (past perfect).	Using expanded noun phrases to describe and specify (Y2).
Term 3	Using modal verbs or adverbs to indicate degrees of possibility.	Using expanded noun phrases to convey complicated information concisely.	Using and punctuating direct speech (Y3/4).
Term 4	Using relative clauses beginning with **who**, **which**, where, when, whose, **that** or using an implied (i.e. omitted) pronoun. Using commas to clarify meaning and avoid ambiguity in writing.	Using modal verbs or adverbs to indicate degrees of possibility.	Using fronted adverbials (Y3/4). Using commas after fronted adverbials (Y3/4).
Term 5	Using the perfect form of verbs to mark relationships of time and cause (future perfect).	Using the perfect form of verbs to mark relationships of time and cause (past perfect).	Using the present perfect form of verbs in contrast to the past tense (Y3/4).
Term 6	Using relative clauses beginning with who, which, **where, when, whose,** that or using an implied (i.e. omitted) pronoun. Using brackets, dashes or commas to indicate parenthesis.	Using relative clauses beginning with **who, which**, where, when, whose, **that** or using an implied (i.e. omitted) pronoun.	Using subordination and co-ordination (Y2). Extending the range of sentences with more than one clause by using a wider range of conjunctions (Y3/4).

Year 6

	Introduce	Practise	Revisit
Term 1	Using relative clauses beginning with who, which, where, when, whose, that or **using an implied (i.e. omitted) pronoun.**	Using expanded noun phrases to convey complicated information concisely. Using brackets, dashes or commas to indicate parenthesis.	Using fronted adverbials (Y3/4). Using commas after fronted adverbials (Y3/4).
Term 2	Using passive verbs to affect the presentation of information in a sentence. Using hyphens to avoid ambiguity.		Choosing nouns or pronouns appropriately for clarity and cohesion and to avoid repetition (Y3/4).
Term 3	Using the perfect form of verbs to mark relationships of time and cause (perfect progressive forms). Using semi-colons, colons or dashes to mark boundaries between independent clauses.	Using the perfect form of verbs to mark relationships of time and cause (past and future perfect).	
Term 4	Recognising vocabulary and structures that are appropriate for formal speech and writing, including subjunctive forms. Using a colon to introduce a list. Punctuating bullet points consistently.	Using semi-colons, colons or dashes to mark boundaries between independent clauses. Using passive verbs to affect the presentation of information in a sentence.	
Term 5	Use assessment to identify key areas that may need revisiting.		
Term 6		Recognising vocabulary and structures that are appropriate for formal speech and writing, including subjunctive forms. Using semi-colons, colons or dashes to mark boundaries between independent clauses. Using passive verbs to affect the presentation of information in a sentence.	

Reference

Department for Education (DfE) (2014) *National curriculum in England: framework for key stages 1 to 4*. London: Department for Education.

CHAPTER 3.2
RECOGNISING VOCABULARY AND STRUCTURES THAT ARE APPROPRIATE FOR FORMAL SPEECH AND WRITING, INCLUDING SUBJUNCTIVE FORMS

Essential knowledge

This statutory requirement is all about developing a strong understanding of how to speak and write formally. It is, however, interesting to note that the only technique that has been explicitly identified in order to achieve this is the use of subjunctive forms. Therefore, it is essential to pause to think about the many other techniques that support formal speech and writing. When reading the above statutory requirement, it would be easy to make the mistake that this statement is all about using the subjunctive form when, in fact, it is about much more than that.

Therefore, when teaching this statutory requirement, all the following formal techniques need to be considered.

Some modal verbs in certain grammatical structures – for example:

* *Should it rain, we may have to cancel the picnic.*
* *This village would appear normal . . .*
* *Most people might ask . . .*

The subjunctive – for example:

* *If I were to come in . . .*
* *Were they to come in . . .*
* *They requested that he leave immediately.*

Some use of abstract nouns and noun phrases used as the subject of the verb – for example:

- *Darkness was being whispered in . . .*
- *. . . full of despair.*
- *Of course, the most significant matter of evacuation is . . .*

Some passive constructions – for example:

- *It is widely believed that . . .*
- *You are provided with a life-jacket . . .*
- *Flocks of sheep have been taken . . .*

The personal pronoun 'one' – for example:

- *One should not be concerned about . . .*
- *It is better to do this oneself.*

Vocabulary that is technical, or context-/subject-specific – for example:

- *. . . plea for mercy . . .*
- *. . . oil producers . . . plantations. . . non-sustainable . . .*
- *. . . these are my words of farewell.*

Nominalisation (use of nouns rather than verbs or adjectives) – for example:

> *The arrival of the mysterious stranger caused considerable excitement.*

rather than:

> *We were very excited when the mysterious stranger arrived.*

> *(Standards and Testing Agency, 2016)*

Many of the features listed above are addressed in different statutory requirement statements, so these will be explored fully in the sections that focus on those.

The subjunctive form

The National Curriculum Glossary (DFE, 2014) is particularly unhelpful when trying to understand the subjunctive. It states:

> *In some languages, the inflections of a verb include a large number of special forms which are used typically in subordinate clauses, and are called subjunctives. English has very few such forms and those it has tend to be used in rather formal speech.*

Probably the most useful point to be gleaned from this is that there are few subjunctive forms that are used in English. It does not explain what the subjunctive is, or why or when it would be used.

There are many different explanations to be found elsewhere; however, the following is helpful as it is linked to different types of sentences and ways of expressing ideas:

The subjunctive mood is the verb form used to express a wish, a suggestion, a command, or a condition that is contrary to fact.

The best way to explore these is by looking at some examples. The most likely form that the children may come across is the following:

*I wish **it were** still here.*
*I wish **he were** still here.*

Generally, the grammatical agreement with the third person singular pronoun *he, she* or *it* should be *was* – for example:

He was cold.
It was a good film.

However, when using the subjunctive, instead of using *it was*, we would use *it were*:

If he were cold, he would need to wear a coat.
If it were a good film, I would have stayed until the end.

This is the same for all first-person agreement with the verb 'to be':

If I were rich, I would not need to worry about anything.

As these examples show, when using the subjunctive with first- or third-person subjects, *was* is changed to *were*. It is also useful to note that in these examples, the subjunctive is used in the subordinate clause rather than the main clause.

There are two other ways that create the subjunctive form:

*The architect suggested that the site **be** visited soon.*

be is used instead of *is* or *are*.

*Mrs Jones suggests that Rachel **work** on her project every day this week.*

Instead of Rachel *works*, we drop the *s* and say Rachel *work*.

Out of the three subjunctive forms suggested above, the first one is the one that children are most likely to come across.

Introductory teaching

The subjunctive

Write two sentences on the board:

*If Tom **was** in charge of the school, he would introduce longer playtimes.*
*If Tom **were** in charge of the school, he would introduce longer playtimes.*

Ask the children to tell you what is different about the two sentences. They should spot that one sentence contains the word 'was' and the other contains the word 'were'.

Explain that generally, if we are writing in third-person singular, we would use 'was' with the subject and we would not use 'were'. However, there are some occasions when we want to talk about something that is not actually fact. It may be a wish, a suggestion or a possibility. In these cases, there is a particular verb form that is called the subjunctive. The second sentence demonstrates one way of using the subjunctive.

Explain that we can use the subjunctive here because what is said is not fact. Tom is not actually in charge of the school. If he were, we would have to write:

Tom was in charge of the school. He introduced longer playtimes.

However, as this is not actually fact but merely a possibility, then the subjunctive should be used.

Show another example:

*If I **was** rich, I would buy one hundred cars.*
*If I **were** rich, I would buy one hundred cars.*

Again, ask the children to work out the difference – 'was' or 'were'?

Looking back at the previous set of examples, can the children determine which one is correct? They should identify the second sentence: it uses the subjunctive form because the person writing the sentence is not actually rich, but is just expressing a desire. This one is written in first-person singular and, as it is the subjunctive form, uses 'I were' rather than 'I was'.

Write another sentence up – this one expresses a fact, so would be incorrect if the subjunctive were used. Ask the children to change it so that it does require the subjunctive form and that it is written correctly.

Johnny English was a good spy. He was successful on all his missions.

They should write:

If Johnny English were a good spy, he would be successful on all his missions.

The children may need to work on a few more examples to fully consolidate this. Other examples could be:

Tom learns his spellings. He always gets top marks in the tests.
(If Tom were to learn his spellings, he would get top marks in the tests.)
Jemma goes to netball practice every day. She gets to play in all the matches.
(If Jemma went to netball practice every day, she would play in all the matches.)
Natalie goes to bed early. She never oversleeps in the morning.
(If Natalie went to bed early, she would never oversleep in the morning.)

End the session by asking the children to explain when they would use the subjunctive.

They should use it when they talk or write about something that is not actually fact; it may be a wish, a suggestion or a possibility.

LITTLE AND OFTEN ACTIVITIES

CHANGING SENTENCES USING THE SUBJUNCTIVE

Share some sentences that should be written using the subjunctive and ask the children to change them so that they are written correctly – for example:

- *If I was you, I would make sure I was on time.*
- *If Tom was on time more often, he would not get into so much trouble.*
- *I wish it was December because it would soon be Christmas.*
- *If it was not for Mum's help, Charlotte would have failed her test.*
- *If the train was on time for once, everyone would be happy.*

SPOTTING THE SUBJUNCTIVE

Share some sentences with the children and ask them to identify whether they use the subjunctive form or not – for example:

- *If Dion was more careful, he would have less accidents.*
- *If Emily were braver, she could dive off the top board at the swimming pool.*
- *If I was in charge of the library, everyone would get free books.*
- *If a lion were smaller, it would not be able to run so fast.*

Point out that the two sentences which do not use the subjunctive should do. Ask the children to change them so that they do use the subjunctive.

ABSTRACT NOUNS

Abstract nouns refer to intangible things that you cannot actually see or touch. They refer to feelings, actions, ideas and qualities.

Provide the children with a list of words and ask them to change them into abstract nouns – for example:

Chaotic would become *chaos*.

Below are some words that can be changed into abstract nouns, although it would be easy to think of many more.

happy (happiness)	*empty (emptiness)*
brave (bravery)	*negative (negativity)*
hate (hatred)	*jealous (jealousy)*
tolerant (tolerance)	*wise (wisdom)*

(Continued)

(Continued)

warm (warmth)   *angry (anger)*

helpful (helpfulness)   *able (ability)*

disturb (disturbance)   *forgive (forgiveness)*

inform (information)   *educate (education)*

Once children have created the abstract nouns, the challenge is to use them in a sentence. For example:

- *Education is important for all children.*
- *The information provided helped people to make a decision.*

This is helping to create nominalisation, which is when nouns are used instead of verbs or adjectives.

CREATING NOMINALISATION

Ask the children to alter the sentences below by using nouns instead of the identified verbs and adjectives. For example:

- *The **brave** prince was rewarded.*
- *The prince was rewarded for his **bravery**.*

Ask the children to try changing the following:

*The room was very **warm**.* (warmth)	*Parents are **obliged** to keep their children safe from danger.* (obligation)
*It was obvious that the fighter was **strong**.* (strength)	*Everyone is **required** to sign the trip consent form.* (requirement)
*Everyone was **disturbed** by the noisy planes.* (disturbance)	*Most animals need to learn skills to help them **survive** in the wild.* (survival)
*Tom is **able** to play the violin to a high standard.* (ability)	

Finding examples in reading

The subjunctive form appears surprisingly often in books and not always in formal writing. There are a number of poems and songs where it is used, as well as in some delightful books for young children.

Share some of the examples with the class and ask them to identify where the subjunctive is used:

If I were rich, I'd have the time that I lack
To sit in the synagogue and pray.

And maybe have a seat by the Eastern wall.

And I'd discuss the holy books with the learned men, several hours every day.

That would be the sweetest thing of all.

('If I were a Rich Man', *Fiddler on the Roof*)

What can I give Him, poor as I am?

If I were a shepherd, I would bring a lamb;

If I were a Wise Man, I would do my part;

Yet what I can I give Him: give my heart.

('In the Bleak Midwinter', Christina Rossetti)

There are a couple of poetry books that also provide good examples of this form of the subjunctive.

If I were a Book is a wonderful publication written by José Jorge Letria and illustrated by André Letria. On every page there is a possibility or desire expressed based on 'If I were a book . . . – for example:

'If I were a book, I would not want to know at the beginning how my story ends.'

'If I were a book, I'd be happy to wind up on a desert island with a passionate reader.'

Not only is this book full of beautiful ideas, it would be very useful to explore in order to promote reading for pleasure. The class could use this for the basis of a jointly compiled book, with each child writing their own 'If I were a book . . .' idea.

One other poetry book I would recommend is *If I were in Charge of the World (and Other Worries)* by Judith Viorst (1984). The first poem in the book is the same as the title and provides a good model for using the subjunctive form.

As the subjunctive is an indicator of more formal speech and writing, it is worth trying to locate examples in factual non-fiction writing. However, there are occasions in books where the subjunctive should have been used but has not.

The book *If . . .* , written by David J Smith and illustrated by Steve Adams (2014), is one such example. As the cover states, this book is *a mind-bending way of looking at big ideas and numbers.* It is an interesting book but, from a grammatical point of view, lacks the subjunctive. Ask the children to go through the book and identify where the subjunctive should have been used – for example:

If the Milky Way was shrunk to the size of a dinner plate . . .

If the history of the last 3000 years was condensed into one month . . .

There are at least ten examples in the book where the subjunctive could have been used. Challenge the children to find them and to rewrite the sentences using the subjunctive correctly.

Looking for examples of nominalisation in reading

A good place to look for examples of nominalisation is an encyclopedia. Provide a factual passage and ask the children to identify any abstract nouns that have created nominalisation. Below are examples from the *DK Why? Encyclopedia* (2014). Each contains one example of an abstract noun:

What is a tornado?

Tornadoes are powerful, swirling, spinning winds that sometimes form beneath a storm cloud. Wherever they touch land, tornadoes sweep across the ground leaving behind a trail of destruction. A tornado can last for just a few seconds or more than an hour.

Why do volcanoes erupt?

Volcanoes can erupt when pressure deep underground forces hot, liquid rock (called magma) from inside the Earth up to the surface. An eruption blasts out clouds of ash and molten (melted) rock into the air around it.

Applying in writing

There is a large collection of children's textured picture board books. All the titles are similar and all use the conjunctive form 'If I were . . .'
One example is 'If I were a sheep' by Anne Wilkinson (2008).

If I were a sheep . . .

My coat would be woolly

My knees would be knobbly

My ears would be velveting

My nose would be wrinkly

If I were a sheep and I couldn't get to sleep

I would lie on the hill and count sheep!

Each double page contains a separate idea with a texture for the young reader to feel.
The children could have a go at devising their own 'If I were' stories and making them into board books with pictures and textures that would be suitable for young children. If the school has a nursery, these could be shared with the children there.
It is also worth pointing out that by making these books, the children would also be using **modal verbs** which are explored later in Chapter 3.6.
The children could also write more formally by preparing a speech – for example:

If I were prime minister . . .

or

If I were in charge of Christmas . . .

Not only should they attempt to use the subjunctive form, but also the range of features that contribute to formal writing as discussed above.

Factual writing

After reading the book *If . . .*, as discussed above, encourage the children to write their own 'If . . .' books, perhaps by making up some weird and wonderful imaginary facts of their own. They could collect some facts about school or the village or town in which they live; alternatively, they could make up their own country or planet on which to base their ideas.

As well as encouraging the use of the subjunctive, they need to ensure that they are able to maintain a formal tone throughout the piece using a range of techniques – for example:

- technical and formal vocabulary
- the passive form of verbs
- avoiding some contractions
- use of abstract nouns for nominalisation

TERMINOLOGY

- formal
- informal
- subjunctive
- nominalisation
- abstract noun

Reference

Department for Education (DfE) (2014) *National curriculum in England: framework for key stages 1 to 4*. London: Department for Education.

CHAPTER 3.3

USING PASSIVE VERBS TO AFFECT THE PRESENTATION OF INFORMATION IN A SENTENCE

Essential knowledge

In order to understand passive verbs and to form passive constructions, children need to understand *subjects* and *verbs*. The *subject* is always the person or the thing that the sentence or the clause is about. The *verb* tells you what is happening in the sentence.

Children also need to be able to distinguish between *active* and *passive* sentences.

In sentences that use active verbs, the subject performs the action; however, in sentences that use passive verbs, the subject doesn't do anything but has something done to it – for example:

Alice presented the show. (active)

The show was presented by Alice. (passive)

In the first sentence, Alice is the subject and she has done something. The show is the object because that is the thing that is affected by the action. In the second sentence, Alice is no longer the subject: the subject is now the show which has not actively done anything. However, it has had an action performed on it by Alice.

Sometimes, people mistakenly believe that when transforming an active sentence into a passive one, the subject moves its position in the sentence, but this is not the case; what happens is that the subject changes.

The National Curriculum Glossary (DfE, 2014) says this about active and passive verbs:

The sentence It was eaten by our dog is the passive of Our dog ate it.

A passive is recognisable from:

- *The past participle form eaten*
- *The normal object (it) turned into the subject*
- *The normal subject (our dog) turned into an optional preposition phrase with by at its head*
- *The verb be (was), or some other verb such as get.*

Contrast active

A verb is not 'passive' just because it has a passive meaning: it must be the passive version of an active verb.

Some useful points are made in this guidance; however, some parts do require a little more explanation.

When talking about participles, it is not easy to find a straightforward explanation. Basically, there are present participles and past participles. These do not necessarily relate to writing in the present tense or in the past tense; it is more to do with how they are used.

The present participle ends in *-ing* and therefore is part of the progressive form of verbs (the progressive form is introduced in Year 2).

The past participle often ends with *-ed*, although there are many irregular forms such as *-t*, *-en*. These are often used to make perfect forms of verbs. (The present perfect is introduced in Years 3 and 4 – see Chapter 2.3).

Where the verbs *be* and *was* are mentioned, these are used as auxiliary verbs. These are verbs that are used with other verbs in order to add extra meaning to the main verb.

As well as understanding and recognising passive verbs in sentences, it is useful for children to know why and when to use them.

As stated in the statutory requirement, using passive verbs does affect the presentation of information in a sentence. Consider this statement when thinking about the examples already provided:

Alice presented the show. (active)
The show was presented by Alice. (passive)

In the active sentence, the subject is Alice and, therefore, the writer is telling the audience about Alice. However, in the passive sentence, the subject is the show. In this case, the audience is primarily being informed about the show rather than about Alice. Therefore, in order to understand active and passive forms, children need to understand about the subject within a sentence. If they do not understand this, it will be difficult for them to alter their sentence constructions.

Why use the passive form, though? First, it does often add an air of formality to writing, which is why it is more likely to be found in formal factual writing rather than in narratives or more informal writing. It can enable the writer to sound quite authoritative.

Another reason for using the passive form is when the writer decides that the person performing the action is not important – for example:

Pyramids were built thousands of years ago.

In this sentence, the subject is obviously 'pyramids'. The important information is when they were built. It is not necessary to say that they were built by the Ancient Egyptians, as this should be obvious to the reader.

The passive form may also be used when the writer does not know who performed the action – for example:

Several robberies were committed over the weekend.

This sentence could quite possibly appear in a newspaper report at a time when the thieves have not yet been caught and are therefore unknown. Rather than writing an active sentence such as:

Robbers committed several robberies over the weekend.

which would sound quite weak, the writer can transform it to a passive sentence and be able to leave out the unknown robbers.

Writers may also choose to use passive verbs when they want to affect the way the reader thinks by changing the focus of the sentence. Consider the following two examples:

Tom ate all the ice cream. (active)

All the ice cream was eaten by Tom. (passive)

In the first sentence, which is active, the subject is Tom. This makes Tom the focus of the sentence and it sounds like the writer is directing blame at Tom for eating all the ice cream. In the second sentence, which is passive, the subject is the ice cream. By forming this passive construction, the focus is now on the ice cream and the fact it has all been eaten. The writer can even choose not to tell the reader who has eaten it all which could not happen in an active sentence.

The above examples are intended to illustrate some of the many reasons why the passive form of verbs might be used. It is important that, when learning about this, the children not only know how to construct passive forms, but that they understand how they affect the presentation of information and why the writer may have chosen that form.

Introductory teaching

Write a straightforward active sentence on the board – for example:

Charlotte kicked the ball.

Ask the children to tell you who the sentence is about – Charlotte. Therefore, Charlotte is the subject within the sentence.

Then ask what Charlotte is doing – kicking the ball. The verb in the sentence is 'kicked' – the word that tells you what's happening.

Explain that this is an **active sentence** as the subject (Charlotte) is doing something (kicking the ball).

Tell the children that there could be a different way of writing this, and write up:

The ball was kicked by Charlotte.

In this new sentence, Charlotte is no longer the subject; the subject is now the ball. However, the ball is not actually doing anything; it is having something done to it, thus making it a **passive sentence**.

Also point out that in this straightforward passive sentence, two words have been added – 'was' and 'by'. These are key words when we use a passive sentence, but we still want to mention who performed the action.

'Was' has been added because the sentence is written in the past tense; if it were written in the present tense, we would need to add 'is'.

Provide a new active sentence:

Danny cleaned the bathroom.

Ask the children to first identify the subject (Danny) and the verb (cleaned) and then change it from an active sentence to a passive one. They should write:

The bathroom was cleaned by Danny.

Ask the children to explain to a partner what they have done. They should explain that they have changed the subject in the sentence and that it is now the bathroom instead of Danny. They have also added the two words – 'was' and 'by' – to show that it is past tense and who performed the action.

Ask them to do the same with some more active sentences:

The science teacher conducted the experiment.

Many tourists visited Spain this year.

Most world leaders signed the treaty.

Each time the children change an active sentence into a passive one, encourage them to explain what they have done.

Finally, to consolidate their understanding, ask the children to write down the difference between an active and passive sentence. The most important point to draw out is the way the different types of sentence affects the way that the information is presented because it changes what or who the sentence is about.

LITTLE AND OFTEN ACTIVITIES

ACTIVE OR PASSIVE

Share several sentences with the children. All they need to do is to determine whether the sentence is an active sentence (using active verbs) or a passive sentence (using passive verbs). Not all passive sentences include the person or thing that performed the action – for example:

Many people visited the museum this year. (active)
These bottles cannot be opened easily. (passive)
Road workers repaired the potholes in the high street. (active)
Baby kangaroos are carried by their mothers in their pouches. (passive)
Male penguins look after the baby chicks. (active)
The kittens had been abandoned by their mother. (passive)

For each sentence, ask the children to explain why the sentence is either active or passive. (It is active if the subject is performing an action; it is passive if the subject is having an action performed on it.)

CHANGING ACTIVE SENTENCES TO PASSIVE

Share some active sentences with the children and ask them to change them to passive. Start with some straightforward ones first – for example:

Imran made the tea.
Grandpa read the book.

In both these examples, the children should be able to form new sentences using passive verbs:

The tea was made by Imran.
The book was read by Grandpa.

Ask the children to identify the subject in the active sentence and then in the passive sentence. By asking them to do this on a regular basis, it will help to them to understand about the subject in a sentence and also to understand that when transforming an active sentence to a passive, the subject changes.

It is worth pointing out that both these examples are quite basic and do not have much impact on the reader. However, they provide a starting point from which to move on to more useful constructions.

The following are examples where transforming the active to the passive form may be more effective:

Children cannot open these bottles easily.
My son ate all the homemade cookies.
Corrosion had damaged the hull of the ship.
Khalid painted the spare bedroom.
Rachel iced two hundred cakes for the charity sale.

As before, ask the children to identify the subject in both the active and the passive sentence.

They also need to consider how the focus of the sentence changes and whether they would need to say who or what had performed the action in the passive sentence – for example:

Children cannot open these bottles easily. (active)

This should change to:

These bottles cannot be easily opened by children. (passive)

At this point, you could have a discussion with the children as to whether they think they should keep 'by children' or leave that information out. Their answers might depend on what type of bottles they are talking about. If, for example, they are medicine bottles, it is extremely useful to point out that it is children who cannot open them.

The following two examples often cause confusion as they are multi-clause sentences. In order to successfully change these from active sentences to passive ones, the children

(Continued)

(Continued)

need to identify the main clause as that is the one that changes. The subordinate clause remains the same.

Many tourists were visiting Stonehenge while I was there.
When she arrived, the changes amazed her.

The passive constructions should be:

Stonehenge was visited by many tourists while I was there.
When she arrived, she was amazed by the changes.

CAN EVERY ACTIVE SENTENCE BE CHANGED TO USE PASSIVE VERBS?

In this activity, ask the children to assess whether the passive verb form is always an effective way of presenting information. Present the following sentences to the children and, first, ask them whether it is possible to change them to use the passive verb form. It will not be possible for all the sentences. It is only possible to change sentences that have an object as well as a subject.

Once they have decided that a sentence can be changed, ask them to change it and then to assess whether it works or if it would have been better to leave it as an active sentence.

The entire school watched the opening ceremony.
Carys strolled along the road.
Medhi laughed loudly.
Kevin McCloud presents 'Grand Designs'.
Ruby was the fastest swimmer in the school.
Swallows Class will visit the museum tomorrow.
Tom ate everything on his plate.

Only the sentences in bold can be changed effectively from active to passive.

Finding examples in reading

News reports are useful in trying to locate examples of passive verbs affecting the presentation of information. One useful source is the bbc newsround website (**www.bbc.co.uk/ newsround**) which offers many short news stories. These are being updated all the time, so there should be a continual source of factual, informative writing.

Share an extract with the children – for example, this piece from September 2018 about Hurricane Florence:

Tropical storm Florence continues to cause tremendous damage to parts of the Carolinas where it first struck as a Hurricane on Friday.

*Crawling inland at 35mph, **it is feared** more **communities will be flooded by the rain** it is bringing with it.*

"This system is unloading epic amounts of rainfall," North Carolina Governor Roy Cooper said on Saturday.

He told residents in areas affected not to return to their homes as it is still dangerous, with "all roads in the state at risk of floods".

US media reports at least 12 people have died in the storm.

*President Donald Trump has declared it as a disaster, which means **more money can be distributed to help areas** most in need. **He is expected** to visit the region next week.*

There are four examples of passive verbs being used: challenge the children to find them and to discuss how effective they are. They should notice that in some of these, the person or thing performing the action is not mentioned.

Encyclopedias often provide examples of the passive voice in their factual entries. The DK *Why? Encyclopedia* (2014) provides many examples for the children to find. Quite often it is the first sentence that introduces the topic that is formed by using the passive.

What makes a car go?

Most cars are powered by an engine *that uses petrol or diesel, which are liquid fuels. The car's engine burns this fuel to move a system of roads and cogs, which turn the car's wheels and make it go.*

(DK *Why? Encyclopedia*, 2014, p125)

Ask the children to identify the passive construction and to notice where it appears in the passage. Challenge them to look through different encyclopedia entries to locate passive constructions and to particularly notice if they are introductory sentences.

The following is a particularly useful example as it contains many passive constructions that support the authoritative tone of an encyclopaedia and also demonstrate how some effective passive constructions do not mention the person or people who have performed the action.

What's inside a pyramid?

The Great Pyramid of Giza, *on the banks of the River Nile,* ***was built as a tomb to contain the body of Egypt's ruler, the pharaoh Khufu.*** *The huge pyramid is built from more than two million stone blocks stacked into 200 layers.*

When it was first built, ***the stones were covered*** *with a layer of polished limestone.*

The Middle Chamber was originally called the Queen's Chamber. ***It is thought to have contained*** *a statue of the king as well as items such as furniture, tools and weapons.*

Today's entrance was created *in the year 820 CE.* ***It was made by robbers*** *when they were breaking into the pyramid.*

(DK *Why? Encyclopedia*, 2014, p88)

There are numerous examples in these different extracts about the pyramids. Children could list all the examples that they have found and discuss how effective they are. It is important to note that, in both examples, not all sentences are written using passive verbs as this would start to sound clumsy. A good balance of different types of sentences is always needed.

Applying in writing

Factual writing

It is useful for children to be taught how to spot opportunities for using passive verbs when presenting information. Encourage them to do this in their own work when writing formally. However, in order to help them to do so, provide real-life examples where they can be challenged to change the writing to include more passive verbs.

The extract below is from the bbc newsround website (**www.bbc.co.uk/newsround**) and is taken from a report: Five facts about NASA's new space laser:

> Once in orbit around the earth, <u>the laser will fire 10,000 shots of light per second!</u> It's a technique called photon counting. A 'photon' is a particle of light.
>
> Each shot fired by the laser hits the earth's surface and bounces back. The time it takes for the light to bounce back to the satellite helps scientists work out distance and height of the reflecting surface.
>
> Cathy Richardson, who has helped develop the instrument explains:
>
> "<u>We fire about a trillion photons in every shot.</u> We get about one back . . . We can time that one photon when it comes back just as accurately as when it left the instrument. And from that <u>we can calculate a distance to about half a centimetre on the Earth.</u>"

The underlined words are the possible places where active can be turned into passive verbs, which would also help the children make their writing more impersonal.

Encyclopedia entries

Challenge the children to make up a new insect that has just been discovered. Ask them to create several facts about this new creature ready to write a new encyclopedia entry. They will need to write one or two paragraphs. The challenge is to open the writing with a sentence that contains a passive verb. A further challenge is to include some more sentences constructed in the same way – but not too many.

TERMINOLOGY

- active
- passive
- subject
- verb
- sentence
- clause
- participle

Reference

Department for Education (DfE) (2014) *National curriculum in England: framework for key stages 1 to 4*. London: Department for Education.

CHAPTER 3.4

USING THE PERFECT FORM OF VERBS TO MARK RELATIONSHIPS OF TIME AND CAUSE

Essential knowledge

Children will already know much about verb forms by the time they reach Year 5. They will know about the *past and present tenses* and will have been introduced to the *progressive* form of both the past and present tense in Year 2. This will have been followed by the introduction of *the present perfect in contrast to the past tense* in Years 3 and 4. This new statutory requirement – using the perfect form of verbs to mark relationships of time and cause – will help them to develop a wider understanding of how tenses work and the different verb forms. By the end of Key Stage 2, they should have been introduced to several other variations of the perfect form of verbs.

The National Curriculum Glossary (DfE, 2014) provides the following explanation:

> *The perfect form of a verb generally calls attention to the consequences of a prior event; for example, he has gone to lunch implies that he is still away, in contrast with he went to lunch. 'Had gone to lunch' takes a past time point (i.e. when we arrived) as its reference point and is another way of establishing time relations in a text.*

This really is not very helpful, so it is necessary to provide an explanation that children will understand. Perhaps a simpler way to explain perfect tenses is to say that we use the present perfect, past perfect and future perfect verb tenses when talking or writing about actions that are completed now (in the present), or by a specific time either in the past or the future.

One reason for using the past perfect is to talk about something that happened in the past before something else – for example:

I had completed my homework just before I left for school.

The present perfect, as already discussed in Chapter 2.3, can be used to explain something that has happened but has no fixed time or is still happening now – for example:

Mrs Patel has been a teacher for six years.

The future perfect can be used to express an action which is not yet complete but will be at some fixed point in the future – for example:

Danny will have finished his project by the weekend.

There are other reasons for using the perfect tenses, but it is best to focus on just a few.

There are twelve different verb forms that they may come across in their reading and use in their speech and their writing. These are listed in the table below, each with a simple example.

Past simple	Present simple	Future simple
I walked	I walk	I will walk
Past progressive	**Present progressive**	**Future progressive**
I was walking	I am walking	I will be walking
Past perfect	**Present perfect**	**Future perfect**
I had walked	I have walked	I will have walked
Past perfect progressive	**Present perfect progressive**	**Future perfect progressive**
I had been walking	I have been walking	I will have been walking

Apart from the past simple and present simple, the rest of these verb forms are created through a combination of an *auxiliary* verb and a *lexical* verb.

Auxiliary verbs are often referred to as 'helping verbs'. In the examples above, words such as *am*, *was* and *have* are auxiliary verbs; these help to express the full force of the verb and to establish the verb form. The modal verb *will* is used with the future tenses.

Lexical verbs are the verbs that have more meaning; they are the main verbs in a sentence.

The most common and useful of these is the past perfect, which will be the main focus of this chapter, although the others will also be addressed.

Introductory teaching

Ask the children to tell you what they have already learned about *verbs*. Responses should include:

*   *They are the words that tell you what is happening in a sentence.*
*   *They can have different tenses.*
*   *Verbs have a progressive form.*
*   *The present perfect can be used in contrast to the past tense.*

If children are unsure of any of the above, they should be revisited before introducing other perfect forms of verbs.

Ask the children what they can tell you about the present perfect form of verbs:

- *It can be used in contrast to the past tense.*
- *It is made up of two parts – for example, have + walked.*
- *It is the first word – have/has – that tells you that it is present tense.*
- *It is a perfect verb because it refers to a completed action.*

Provide the children with a sentence written in the past tense and ask them to change it to the present perfect form – for example:

Sam walked to school every day. (past tense)

Sam has walked to school every day. (present perfect)

Make sure that the children can write using the present perfect form before moving on to introducing the past perfect. You may need to ask them to write a few more examples.

Display the present perfect example:

Sam has walked to school every day.

Tell the children that you are going to change the sentence slightly in order to write it using the past perfect form. Ask if anyone can think which word needs to be changed in order to do this.

Either let the children tell you or, if they cannot work it out, tell them that the word that is going to be changed is *has.*

Has is a present tense verb and, so that the past perfect can be formed, this word needs to be written in the past tense – *had.* Therefore, the new sentence becomes:

Sam had walked to school every day.

Provide a few more present perfect sentences for the children to change to past perfect – for example:

Jamie has visited his grandparents.

Serena has eaten all the biscuits.

Explain, that if we say that Jamie *has visited* his grandparents, this has happened very recently; however, if he *had visited* his grandparents, that would have happened at some time in the past. It is helped if we place an adverbial at the end of each sentence to reinforce this – for example:

Jamie has visited his grandparents today.

Jamie had visited his grandparents last year.

We could have just written:

Jamie visited his grandparents last year (using the past simple).

However, we can use the past perfect to say that an action happened in the past before something else happened – for example:

Jamie had visited his grandparents before they moved away.

Provide a couple more examples for the children to work on, changing the present perfect to the past perfect:

Patrick has read all the books in the library.
Jamil has visited France and Italy this year.
They have lost all their matches this season.

Ask the children to change the above sentences from present perfect to past perfect. Can they provide a time adverbial in order to position each one in the past?

Ask the children to change the following sentences from past simple to past perfect. The lexical verbs are irregular; they will need to be changed from *took* to *taken*, and from *drew* to *drawn*.

The burglars took all the jewellery.
Joey drew a map of the route to his house.

To consolidate, ask the children to explain how the past perfect tense is formed, how it is different from the present perfect, and to suggest ideas about when they would use it.

Later, once the past perfect has been introduced and understood, you could use the same strategy to introduce the future perfect or the perfect progressive forms.

LITTLE AND OFTEN ACTIVITIES

PAST, PRESENT OR FUTURE PERFECT?

Provide the children with several different sentences, one at a time. For each one, ask them to decide whether the sentence is written as past perfect, present perfect or future perfect. The children could devise actions for indicating each one – for example:

- Pointing over their shoulder to indicate past perfect.
- Pointing to themselves for present perfect.
- Pointing forward for future perfect.

For each decision they make, ask the children to explain why. Possible sentences could include:

I have eaten everything on my plate. (present perfect)
I will have completed my homework before going out. (future perfect)
Mum will have bought all the Christmas presents by the start of December. (future perfect)
John had taken his car to the garage to be serviced before he went on holiday. (past perfect)
Charlie has won every race this year. (present perfect)
Tom had raced to the bus stop but still missed the bus. (past perfect)
Toby and Helena have both passed their Grade 2 violin exam. (present perfect)

USING THE PAST, PRESENT AND FUTURE PERFECT FORM OF VERBS

Provide a scenario for the children – for example:

Tom visited his grandparents.

Ask the children to convey this information in three different ways using the past perfect, the present perfect and the future perfect. They should write:

Tom had visited his grandparents. (past perfect)
Tom has visited his grandparents. (present perfect)
Tom will have visited his grandparents. (future perfect)

In order to provide a rationale for each sentence, ask the children to add an adverbial phrase to the end of each one – for example:

Tom had visited his grandparents every Sunday last year. (past perfect)
Tom has visited his grandparents today. (present perfect)
Tom will have visited his grandparents by the end of the week. (future perfect)

Ask the children to explain why each sentence is past, present or future perfect and why they added their phrase at the end.

At different times, ask the children to do the same thing with different scenarios – for example:

Tom repaired his car.
Tom sat his exam.
Ed performed in the music concert.
Amira wrote to the prime minister.
Lisa travelled to Scotland.

For each of the above, ask the children to write the three different sentences using past, present and future perfect tenses and to add an adverbial phrase at the end in order to express time. Ask them to consider how effective each sentence is and whether it makes sense.

FILLING IN THE BLANKS

Provide the children with a sentence with some words missing. The missing word or words will either be *had, have/has* or *will have* and will indicate whether the sentence should be written as past perfect, present perfect or future perfect. The children must decide which one and write the missing word or words on their mini whiteboards. They should always be asked to justify their decision. Possible sentences could be:

(Continued)

(Continued)

Elana	____	*visited her grandparents many times last year. (had)*
Elana	____	*visited her grandparents every week this year. (has)*
Elana	____	*visited her grandparents by the end of the week. (will have)*
The bus	____	*left by the time the boys arrived at the bus stop. (had)*
Amira	____	*never played football before starting secondary school. (had)*
Dora	____	*lived in many places before moving to Scotland. (had/has)*

MIX AND MATCH

This could be carried out as a moving around activity or a paper one.

Share out the clauses and phrases between the children. Every clause is written using a perfect form of the verb. Ideally, whether in a group or working as the whole class, every child should be given either a clause or a phrase. The idea is for children to move around, reading the other clauses and phrases to try to make a match. As soon as a clause and a phrase are joined, the pair must stick together and cannot be joined by any other clause or phrase. Some clauses or phrases may have the option to be joined with more than one other. Ideally, all children will find a match. However, if at the end of the session, there are some unmatched clauses and phrases, encourage the children to consider whether any pairs may change.

Suggested clauses and phrases to use:

Josh will have finished his homework	*by the end of the holiday.*
Cameron has lived here	*last year.*
We will have visited many historic buildings	*tomorrow.*
Tom had visited his grandparents	*by Tuesday.*
Farah will have painted the kitchen	*today.*
Because he had eaten so much food at the party	*three times this week.*
Kiara has practised her clarinet	*many times.*
Tom will have seen the doctor	*every day this week.*
After he had finished his jobs	*by the time his mum gets home.*
I have seen my cousins	*many times before the concert.*
Mrs Jones will have finished all her marking	*Cal played football*
Zoe had earned a lot of money	*for six years.*
Maisie has forgotten her homework	*by five o'clock.*
Sophie had practised the song	*Freddy felt sick.*
Marie has been to Scotland	*from her cake sale last week.*

ENDINGS FOR BEGINNINGS

Provide some sentences that are a mixture of past perfect, present perfect and future perfect. For each sentence, ask the children to think of a suitable adverbial phrase to add to the end of the sentence. Some of these will be to express time whereas others will be to express cause.

Sentences could include:

The lion had raced through the swamp.
The dogs have eaten all the bones.
The mouse will have eaten the cheese.
The passengers have lined up at the entrance.
The monster had crept up the stairs.
The swallows will have flown south.

BEGINNINGS FOR ENDINGS

This is a similar activity to the one above, but this time the adverbial phrases have been provided. For each phrase, the children must think of a past perfect, present perfect or future perfect clause to be written before it. Phrases could include:

this week
by next term
last year
after the bus left
as there was no food left in the cupboard
after they went to bed
because it has run out of petrol

One example could be:

Ali *will have learned* all his times tables *by next term*.

Finding examples in reading

The following extract from *The Secret of Platform 13* by Eva Ibbotson usefully shows how the past perfect form of verbs work in writing in conjunction with other verb forms. Children should be able to spot simple past tense verbs as well as the progressive. Ask the children to identify where the past perfect has been used in the following passage – where one of the characters, Mrs Trottle, is reflecting on recent events – and to discuss its impact.

> *'Ta-ra-ra Boom-de-ray!' sang Mrs Trottle, lathering her round, pink stomach.*
>
> *She felt very pleased with herself for **she had foiled** the kidnappers who were after her darling Raymond. **She had outwitted** the gang; they would never find her babykins now. They would expect her to go to Scotland or to France, **but she had been** too clever for them. The hiding place **she had found** was as safe as houses – and so comfortable.*
>
> (Eva Ibbotson, *The Secret of Platform 13*, 2001, p110)

This is a useful extract as there are several examples of the past perfect, but these are used alongside the past simple and the progressive. This usefully demonstrates that the past perfect would not be solely used when writing a text.

Applying in writing

When writing a story, challenge the children to use a mixture of past tense forms. These should include the past simple, the past progressive, the past perfect and, possibly, the past perfect progressive. The important thing to remember is not to overuse any one of them and to ensure that tense remains consistent.

When reflecting on their writing, children could highlight the different verb forms that they have used in their writing and assess whether there is a good balance.

TERMINOLOGY

- verb
- auxiliary verb
- lexical verb
- perfect

- past
- present
- future
- tense

Reference

Department for Education (DfE) (2014) *National curriculum in England: framework for key stages 1 to 4.* London: Department for Education.

CHAPTER 3.5

USING EXPANDED NOUN PHRASES TO CONVEY COMPLICATED INFORMATION CONCISELY

Essential knowledge

Children will have been introduced to expanded noun phrases in Year 2 to both describe and specify. They will have learned that they can create expanded noun phrases first through placing adjectives between the determiner and the noun; later, they will have learned to create them by adding prepositional phrases. They should have continued to use these through Years 3 and 4. In Years 5 and 6, children need to focus particularly on using expanded noun phrases *to convey complicated information concisely*.

The National Curriculum Glossary (DfE, 2014) explains noun phrases as follows:

> *A noun phrase is a phrase with a noun at its head, e.g. some foxes, foxes with bushy tails.*
>
> *A phrase is a group of words that are grammatically connected so that they stay together, and that expand a single word, called the 'head'. The phrase is a noun phrase if its head is a noun.*

Perhaps this could have been a little more helpful, particularly when considering expanded noun phrases in relation to the above statutory requirement. There is not really much difference between a noun phrase and an expanded noun phrase. A noun phrase could just include a determiner and a noun – for example: some foxes. An expanded noun phrase needs additional information related to the noun. Some people think that an expanded noun phrase must be long and complicated, but that is not the case. Just by adding one adjective– for example, some sly foxes – an expanded noun phrase is created. Most importantly to consider in Years 5 and 6, is how the noun phrase can be used to convey complicated information concisely.

Think about this example that is given in the National Curriculum Glossary (DfE, 2014):

Almost all healthy adult foxes in this area can jump.

Everything that is underlined is part of the expanded noun phrase. The head is the word 'foxes' and all the other words are providing more information about the foxes. It is telling us that:

- *Adult foxes can jump.*
- *They have to be healthy.*
- *These are the healthy adult foxes in the local vicinity; perhaps, in other areas the healthy adult foxes cannot jump.*
- *Not all of them can jump; however, most can.*

As you can see, there is much information provided or suggested here. It is possible to write the information through a series of related sentences; however, it is more concise and fluid to connect all this information in the formation of an expanded noun phrase.

Introductory teaching

First, it is useful to check whether the children can tell you what an expanded noun phrase is – remember that they should have first heard this terminology in Year 2.
Can they tell you:

- What it is? *a group of connected words that provide more information about the noun.*
- Why they have used it so far? *to describe or specify.*
- How it is formed? *by adding adjectives or prepositional phrases to the determiner (if there is one) and the noun.*

Display a couple of straightforward expanded noun phrases:

The beautiful butterfly
The red spotted butterfly

Tell the children that one of these expanded noun phrases is more likely to be used to specify than the other one. Which is it? (The red spotted butterfly.) Can they explain why? The response should include that there is likely to be at least one more butterfly of a different colour or with a different pattern. This expanded noun phrase can obviously also be used to describe.

It is worth pointing out that the beautiful butterfly could also be used to specify, but only if there was an ugly butterfly in the same location. However, this is highly unlikely, as we don't often think of butterflies as ugly.

Explain that the expanded noun phrases that they have just looked at are quite straight-forward and both only contain one extra piece of information. However, some expanded noun phrases contain quite a lot of additional information:

Ask the children to look at the following sentence and identify the expanded noun phrase:

The three small boys wearing matching Christmas jumpers waited at the school gate.

The actual expanded noun phrase here is *the three small boys wearing matching Christmas jumpers* with the word *boys* at the head of the noun phrase.

Ask the children to work out what information is being conveyed in this noun phrase:

- the number of boys
- their size
- what they are wearing
- the theme of the clothes

If this noun phrase is being used to specify, there is also an implication that there is another group of three small boys in the playground who are not wearing matching jumpers (or if they are, they are not wearing Christmas jumpers).

Provide another sentence and ask the children again to identify the expanded noun phrase and to list all the information that is being conveyed within it.

The tired people who docked at Southampton early on Saturday morning had enjoyed their cruise.

The noun phrase includes all the words from the word *morning* with *people* being the head.

The children should be able to tell you that the people:

- are tired;
- they were on a ship that docked in Southampton;
- they docked on Saturday;
- it was early in the morning.

Therefore, this is an example of an expanded noun phrase that conveys several different pieces of information concisely.

Provide the children with a set of information and ask them to connect as much as possible within one expanded noun phrase:

- *a lady*
- *eighty-four years old*
- *grey haired*
- *wears spectacles*
- *worried*

Once they have completed their noun phrase, can they use it in a sentence to make sure that it is coherent?

Finally, ask the children to explain what an expanded noun phrase is and how it helps them to connect different bits of information.

LITTLE AND OFTEN ACTIVITIES

IDENTIFYING NOUN PHRASES IN SENTENCES

Provide the children with a sentence that contains an expanded noun phrase. Ask them to identify it and then unpick all the information contained within it. You could use any of the following sentences or devise your own.

- *A strange object shrouded in mystery* *was found in the pyramid.*
- *The boys discovered **an old tatty envelope containing faded bank notes** in the old abandoned house.*
- ***A well-muscled cat with a long body*** *prowled through the long grass.*
- *We bought **some delicious chocolate from the hotel gift shop**.*
- *Many animals live in **the still, fresh waters of a pond.***
- ***The slime on a frog's skin*** *forms a cocoon to keep water in.*
- *A tortoise has **a tough shell shaped like a dome.***
- ***The lady in the ghastly pink hat who arrived at the station just before me*** *looked completely lost.*

EXPANDED NOUN PHRASES: GUESS THE CHARACTER

All the expanded noun phrases below convey information about characters either from fairy tales or well-known books. Ask the children to work out who they are.

- *an inquisitive girl with a habit of taking things that are not hers* (Goldilocks)
- *a beautiful young princess who cannot stay awake* (Sleeping Beauty)
- *a generous little girl who loves and cares for her grandmother* (Little Red Riding Hood)
- *a talented musician who hates rats (*the Pied Piper)
- *two cruel siblings who think that they are more beautiful than they are* (Cinderella's ugly sisters)
- *a beautiful long-haired girl locked in a tall tower* (Rapunzel)
- *a group of little people who work in a mine* (the seven dwarfs)
- *a young wizard with a prominent scar on his forehead* (Harry Potter)

Once the children have worked out the clues, ask them to create their own expanded noun phrases to describe other characters.

In addition to this, challenge the children to use each expanded noun phrase in a sentence. For example:

A beautiful long-haired girl locked in a tall tower *was desperate to be rescued.*

EXPANDED NOUN PHRASES IN BOOK TITLES

Book titles often contain expanded noun phrases or are made up entirely of an expanded noun phrase – for example, *The Boy in the Striped Pyjamas.*

Provide the children with a list of book titles (or send them to the library with a clipboard) to identify which books contain expanded noun phrases in their titles and to highlight them. Possible book titles include:

The Curious Incident of the Dog in the Night-time (Mark Haddon)	*Goodnight Mister Tom* (Michelle Magorian)
Stig of the Dump (Clive King)	*The Firework-Maker's Daughter* (Philip Pullman)
Where the Wild Things Are (Maurice Sendak)	*Charlie and the Chocolate Factory* (Roald Dahl)
The House at Pooh Corner (AA Milne)	*The Other Side of the Truth* (Beverly Naidoo)
Tell Me No Lies (Malorie Blackman)	*Why the Whales Came* (Michael Morpurgo)
The Voyage of the Dawn Treader (CS Lewis)	*Harry Potter and the Order of the Phoenix* (JK Rowling)

Not all the titles contain expanded noun phrases.

CREATING EXPANDED NOUN PHRASES

There are a variety of ways to encourage the children to create expanded noun phrases.

Display a list of nouns on the board. These could be lists of animals, different types of people or buildings, cars, items of furniture, etc.

Ask the children to choose one and to visualise it in their mind. Then give the children one minute to write down as many words as possible that could possibly go with the noun they have chosen. After that, ask them to look at the ideas they have written down and to select at least three ideas to combine in an expanded noun phrase – for example:

- *eagle*
- *footballer*
- *mouse*
- *snake*
- *cave*

If this task feels too open for the children, provide them with an image. Take a few moments to name different things in the image, thus identifying opportunities for creating expanded noun phrases. Then, as above, ask the children to focus on one thing for a minute, jot down their ideas and then select at least three different ideas that work together well in order to create their expanded noun phrase.

Alternatively, ask the children to look around the classroom and choose something to focus on. It could be absolutely anything from a desk to a paint pot to a book. Give the children one minute to observe their object closely and write down any ideas they think of. Once the minute is up, in the same way as above, ask them to select at least three of their ideas to connect in an expanded noun phrase.

(Continued)

(Continued)

EXPANDED NOUN PHRASES IN LISTS: BEFORE AND AFTER

This is a useful activity to link with punctuation knowledge when looking at how semi-colons are used in punctuating lists of descriptive items.

First provide the children with a simple list – for example:

On my way to school, I went past a tree, a shop, a farm and a petrol station.

This is a rather simple and boring list, and would benefit from more description. Ask the children to think about each item in turn and to add more detail which will create expanded noun phrases – for example:

- *an old oak tree with bare branches*
- *the corner shop where I always buy my favourite magazine*
- *willow Tree farm that has old rusty tractors outside*
- *the BP petrol station in the middle of the roundabout*

Once they have completed the expanded noun phrases, ask them to put them back in a list. This time, though, because the information conveyed is more complicated than the original list, they will need to use semi-colons instead of commas. This will help to separate the different items and to tell the reader that they need to take a slightly longer pause after each item:

On my way to school, I went past an old oak tree with bare branches; the corner shop where I always buy my favourite magazine; Willow Tree farm that has old rusty tractors outside; and the BP petrol station in the middle of the roundabout.

Ask the children to do the same with the following lists:

In my lunchbox, I put a sandwich, a yoghurt, some fruit and a drink.
At the park, Tom went on a swing, a slide, a rope ladder and a climbing frame.
At the zoo, the children saw lions, monkeys, elephants and penguins.

Each time, they need to create expanded noun phrases and not forget to use semi-colons when putting them back in a list.

Finding examples in reading

For children to be able to see how expanded noun phrases can be effective in conveying complicated information concisely, they really need to see how they work in real writing. Below are a couple of extracts where the authors have used expanded noun phrases for this purpose to good effect.

Ask the children to identify the expanded noun phrases and to discuss what information has been conveyed and how effective it is.

*The library at the Academy was a good one. That night Maia sat alone on top of the mahogany library steps, and she read and she read and she read. She read about **the great broad-leaved trees of the rainforest pierced by sudden rays of sun**. She read about **the travellers who had explored the maze of rivers and found a thousand plants and animals that had never been seen before**. She read about **brilliantly coloured birds flashing between the laden branches** – macaws and hummingbirds and parakeets – and butterflies the size of saucers, and **curtains of sweetly scented orchids trailing from the trees**. She read about **the wisdom of the Indians who could cure sickness and wounds that no one in Europe understood.***

(Eva Ebbotson, *Journey to the River Sea*, 2014, p6)

There are so many expanded noun phrases in the passage above that demonstrate how complicated information has been conveyed concisely. The examples also demonstrate rich vocabulary that is worth drawing attention to. Some of the ones that the children could identify include:

- *the great broad-leaved trees of the rainforest pierced by sudden rays of sun*
- *the travellers who had explored the maze of rivers and found a thousand plants and animals that had never been seen before*
- *brilliantly coloured birds flashing between the laden branches*
- *butterflies the size of saucers*
- *curtains of sweetly scented orchids trailing from the trees*
- *the wisdom of the Indians who could cure sickness and wounds that no one in Europe understood.*

Most of these are good examples of where the writer has combined quite complicated information concisely and has made good use of personification.

Ask children to identify the expanded noun phrases in this second extract from *Wolf Brother*:

*Mist floated in the hollows between the mounds, where **the pale, ghostly skeletons of hemlock** reared above his head, and **the purple stalks of dying willowherb** released their eerily drifting down. All around stood **the dark, listening trees**: trees that stayed green all winter, that never slept. In the branches of the tallest yew perched three ravens watching him.*

(Michelle Paver, *Wolf Brother*, 2004, p86)

This extract provides a good example of how expanded noun phrases can be used effectively to describe setting concisely. The notable expanded noun phrases in this example include:

- *the pale, ghostly skeletons of hemlock*
- *the purple stalks of dying willowherb*
- *the dark, listening trees*

This final example also demonstrates how the expanded noun phrase creates personification effectively.

Examples in non-fiction books

Children should also be looking for expanded noun phrases in non-fiction books and in news reports. The example below is from the bbc newsround website (**www.bbc.co.uk/ newsround)** from a report discussing NASA's plans to end a 20-year space mission:

Cassini began its incredible mission to Saturn back in 1997, reaching the ringed planet in 2004.

The aim of the spacecraft was to give the closest, most detailed look at Saturn's rings and its moons.

Amongst its many discoveries Cassini has found new moons orbiting the planet, signs of possible life on existing moons and huge underground oceans spewing fountains of water into space.

The examples for children to find are most noticeable in the final sentence which contains three expanded noun phrases:

- *new moons orbiting the planet*
- *signs of possible life on existing moons*
- *huge underground oceans spewing fountains of water into space*

Applying in writing

Following on from the *Wolf Brother* extract, encourage the children to describe their own settings by using carefully thought-out, expanded noun phrases to combine different information.

You could start by providing an image and giving the children one minute to write down as many words and ideas that they could think of to describe the image. Once they have completed this, ask them to think about which ideas could be combined to work well in a series of expanded noun phrases. Finally, ask them to select some of these to be included in a paragraph that describes their chosen setting.

Another idea, based on the extract from *Journey to the River Sea* by Eva Ibbotson, ask the children to imagine that they have been to a concert where they have heard all their favourite songs. Ask them to describe each song in the same way that the books are described in the extract. For example:

I heard a song about . . .

TERMINOLOGY

- expanded noun phrase
- adjective
- noun
- phrase
- preposition
- prepositional phrase

Reference

Department for Education (DfE) (2014) *National Curriculum in England: framework for key stages 1 to 4.* London: Department of Education.

CHAPTER **3.6**

USING MODAL VERBS OR ADVERBS TO INDICATE DEGREES OF POSSIBILITY

Essential knowledge

The good news about modal verbs is that there are not many of them; in fact, the National Curriculum only lists ten, which makes it relatively easy for children to remember them. They are also words that are often used in speech and writing. The National Curriculum Glossary (DfE, 2014) states the following about modal verbs:

> *Modal verbs are used to change the meanings of other verbs. They can express meanings such as certainty, ability and obligation. The main modal verbs are:*

> will, would, can, could, may, might, shall, should, must and ought.

> *A modal verb only has finite forms and no suffixes (e.g.* I sing – he sings, *but not* I must, he musts).

Children will have already learned that adverbs modify verbs and generally describe when, where or how something happened. However, there are a small number of adverbs that are used to modify adjectives, and these are used to add a degree of intensity to the adjective – for example:

- *That book is **really** easy.*
- *Sam is **very** tall for his age.*
- *The journey was **extremely** boring.*

These types of adverbs can also be used to modify other adverbs – for example:

* *Diksha ran **extremely** quickly.*
* *The tortoise walked **very** slowly.*

Although children need to learn about these, they should not be overused. For example, rather than writing *really quickly*, children should be encouraged to think of a synonym which expresses the same idea more succinctly and appropriately according to the context – for example:

speedily, rapidly, promptly

A useful list of adverbs that indicate degrees of possibility:

quite	*really*	*very*	*extremely*
definitely	*probably*	*possibly*	*normally*
fairly	*absolutely*	*barely*	*completely*
entirely	*hardly*		

Some of these adverbs work with adjectives, some with other adverbs and some with both.

Introductory teaching

Start this session by explaining that although many things in life are possible, some are more possible than others, which is why we need words that help us to express how likely an event may be. Some of the words that help us to express degrees of possibility are called modal verbs.

Write or display the following sentence on the whiteboard:

*It **may** rain tomorrow.*

Ask the children to tell you whether this is quite likely or very likely to happen. Which word is helping them make their decision? Point out that *may* is a modal verb.

Change **may** for **could**:

*It **could** rain tomorrow.*

Is it more or less likely to rain now? It is more likely, but not a certainty that it will rain. Point out that *could* is also a modal verb.

Can the children think of another word to replace 'could' that will make it almost definite that it will rain? They may suggest 'will' or 'shall', both of which are modal verbs:

*It **will** rain tomorrow.*

Explain that we use modal verbs to help to express how likely it is that something may or may not happen.

Provide a list of the following modal verbs:

may, might, can, could, shall, should, will, would, must

Ask the children to choose one to use in a sentence to express the likelihood of the moon being visible in the sky this evening. Ask the children to discuss their choices; they may need to add some extra information – for example:

- *The moon could be visible tonight if there is no cloud.*
- *The moon will be visible tonight as it is a calm evening.*

Discuss why some modal verbs will not work with this event. Finish the session by asking the children to write their own definition of a modal verb.

LITTLE AND OFTEN ACTIVITIES

POSSIBLE OR PROBABLE?

Make sure that a list of modal verbs is visible.

Ask the children to select a modal verb to use in a sentence to express the following – for example:

- *the sun rising tomorrow* (The sun will rise tomorrow.)
- *whether it is going to rain tomorrow*
- *school finishing at 3.30*
- *throwing a six with one die*
- *getting top marks in a spelling test*
- *reading a book later*
- *bumping into an old friend*
- *the sky turning green*

Once the children have written their sentence, ask them to explain why they have selected the modal verb that they used. They may need to add the word *not* – for example, *will not, may not.*

Following on from this, ask the children to come up with their own ideas about things that are possible, probable or certain.

Ask them to write these in sentences using modal verbs.

If the sentence is expressing a possibility, underline the modal verb in blue.

If the sentence is expressing a probability, underline the modal verb in red.

If the sentence is expressing a certainty, underline the modal verb in green.

SCENARIOS

Show a scenario on the board – for example:

The gerbil has escaped.

Ask the children to come up with ideas using modal verbs – for example:

(Continued)

(Continued)

- Someone *may* have accidentally left its cage open.
- It *might* have gnawed through the bars.
- It *could* have dug a tunnel.

Challenge the children to see how many different modal verbs they can use to express different ideas.

The following are other possible scenarios to discuss:

- *The traffic has come to a standstill on the motorway.*
- *The football team has lost all its matches this season.*
- *The car keys have gone missing.*
- *The teacher is extremely happy.*
- *There are a lot of corn flakes on the kitchen floor.*
- *There's a funny beeping sound coming from upstairs.*
- *The road outside our house is wet.*

LINKING WITH THE SUBJUNCTIVE

There are three modal verbs – would, should and could – that are useful to look at when working on the subjunctive (see Chapter 3.2).

Write on the board the start of a sentence that is written using the subjunctive – for example:

If I were prime minister . . .

Challenge the children to complete the sentence in three ways:

If I were prime minister, I would . . .
If I were prime minister, I could . . .
If I were prime minister, I should . . .

Try these with other ideas – for example:

If I were a lion . . .
If I were very rich . . .
If I were the last person on Earth . . .
If I were an astronaut . . .

Always ask the children to discuss their choices and to justify why they have made them.

FILLING IN THE BLANKS

Provide the children with a number of sentences that each have one word missing. That word should either be a modal verb or an adverb that expresses a degree of possibility. Once the children have filled in their missing word, ask them to compare them with others. Have they all filled in the blank with the same word? Ask them to explain their choices.

Possible sentences could include:

Mum _____ be here by now.
I _____ swim by the age of five.
I _____ be home before it gets dark.
I _____ be late this evening.
Nadya _____ like to go to the cinema on Saturday.
I _____ be on time unless the train is late.
I _____ remember my PE kit.
Tom _____ play the clarinet.

It's _____ cold today.
My homework is _____ easy.
Mrs Rose was _____ cross with the class.

Finding examples in reading

The opening of *The Secret of Platform 13* by Eva Ibbotson is not only intriguing, but also a very good example of how modal verbs can be used effectively. Three different modal verbs are used within the first few paragraphs – *might, would* and *could*. Ask the children to spot the modal verbs. *Might* and *could* are both only used once; however, *would* is used on quite a few occasions. Ask the children to think about how these modal verbs contribute to the effectiveness of the writing.

> *If you went into a school nowadays and said to the children: "What is a* gump*?" you* **would** *probably get some very silly answers.*

> *"It's a person without a brain, like a chump," a child* **might** *say. Or:*

> *"It's a camel whose hump has got stuck." Or even:*

> *"It's a kind of chewing gum."*

> *But once this wasn't so. Once every child in the land* **could** *have told you that a gump was a special mound, a grassy bump on the earth, and that in this bump was a hidden door which opened every so often to reveal a tunnel which led to a completely different world.*

> *They* **would** *have known that every country has its own gump and that in Great Britain the gump was in a place called the Hill of the Cross of Kings not far from the River Thames. And the wise children, the ones that read the old stories and listened to the old tales,* **would** *have known more than that. They* **would** *have known that this particular gump opened for exactly nine days every nine years, and not one second longer, and that it was no good changing your mind about coming or going because nothing* **would** *open the door once the time was up.*

> (Eva Ibbotson, *The Secret of Platform 13*, 2001, p1)

This extract will also be useful when exploring how relative clauses are used in writing and linking with the perfect forms of verbs.

Applying in writing

The opening of *The Secret of Platform 13* could also be used as a model for writing, particularly when setting a story in a fantasy world.

Model how the structure of the opening can be applied to a different imaginary place – for example, a *frumble*.

Encourage the children to notice how, in the original extract, the writer has come up with quite a few ideas that rhyme with gump.

Ask them to help you think of words or phrases that rhyme or partly rhyme with frumble – for example:

- apple crumble
- a loud rumble
- rough and tumble
- a bumble bee
- grumble
- humble pie
- jumble sale

The more ideas that they can think of, the more they will have to choose from. Take three of the ideas and show how these can be used in the same way as the different thoughts about a gump are used in *The Secret of Platform 13*. You could model the following:

*If you went into a town nowadays and said to the people: 'What is a frumble?' you **would** probably get some very silly responses.*

*'It's a loud rumbling noise, like thunder,' a child **might** say. Or:*

'It's a delicious apple crumble.' Or even:

'It's a kind of enormous bumble bee.'

*But once this wasn't so. Once every person in the land **could** have told you that a frumble was a secret door that led to the most amazing city that had ever been seen.*

The children could go on to create their own fantasy setting based on the above. Alternatively, they could think of their own made up word and write their own opening to a story based on the same structure.

TERMINOLOGY

- verb
- modal verb
- adverb

Reference

Department for Education (DfE) (2014) *National curriculum in England: framework for key stages 1 to 4*. London: Department for Education.

CHAPTER 3.7

USING RELATIVE CLAUSES BEGINNING WITH WHO, WHICH, WHERE, WHEN, WHOSE, THAT OR USING AN IMPLIED (I.E. OMITTED) PRONOUN

Essential knowledge

Children will have been introduced to subordination in Year 2 using *because, if, when* and *that*. In Years 3 and 4, this will have been worked on further by extending the range of subordinating conjunctions and by being introduced to the term 'clause'. They should know that all sentences will contain at least one clause. If there is more than one clause, these could be a main and a subordinate clause, or two independent clauses. They will also have been introduced to pronouns in Years 3 and 4, and should have a good understanding of personal and possessive pronouns.

Relative clauses are used to give additional information about a noun. They are subordinate clauses as they do not make sense on their own, and can either be embedded within a main clause or placed at the end. If the relative clause is embedded, it generally needs to be demarcated by a comma at both ends. Relative pronouns are used to introduce relative clauses; there are only a small number of these, but whichever one is used depends on what is being referred to – for example:

Who refers to people and, sometimes, pets – for example:

Tom, **who** *has three pet dogs, loves all animals.*

Which refers to animals and things – for example:

Tom's dog, **which** *is called Maisie, has just had five puppies.*

That refers to people, animals and things – for example:

*Tom has a dog **that** has just had five puppies.*

Whose is used in place of the possessive pronoun and must be followed by a noun – for example:

*Tom, **whose** pet dog has just had puppies, is very excited.*

Where and *when* are used with place and time nouns – for example:

*Tom was very excited **when** his pet dog gave birth to five puppies.*

*Tom found his dog in the garage **where** she had just given birth.*

In the National Curriculum Glossary (DfE, 2014) relative clauses have this explanation:

> *A relative clause is a special type of subordinate clause that modifies a noun. It often does this by using a relative pronoun such as who or that to refer back to the noun, though the relative pronoun is often omitted.*

The glossary does not provide any guidance on relative pronouns specifically.

Relative clauses are useful in writing because they help to make writing succinct while adding more detail. However, writing often becomes more fluid if the relative pronoun is taken out, meaning that it is only implied. It is the difference between:

*Rapunzel, **who** was a beautiful princess, was imprisoned at the top of a tall tower.*

And:

Rapunzel, a beautiful princess, was imprisoned at the top of a tall tower.

The first sentence sounds clumsy compared to the second, which also demonstrates how a relative pronoun may not always be necessary. However, there is an implied pronoun because the reader knows who 'a beautiful princess' is referring to.

The relative pronoun cannot always be removed, though. It can only be omitted if the pronoun is the object of the relative clause – for example:

*I haven't played all the games **(that)** I got for my birthday.* (The subject of the relative clause is *I* but *that* is referring to the games; the games are the object in this case.)

and when the relative clause contains a form of the auxiliary verb to be – for example:

*The old man, **(who was)** wearing a bowler hat, strolled round the lake.*

With all types of writing, though, a balance of different types of sentences and clauses is better than too much of any one type.

Introductory teaching

Share the sentences below by having each written on a long strip of card:

Mermaids live at the bottom of the sea.
Ogres prefer to live in swamps.

These are both single-clause sentences. Explain to the children that you want to add some more information about the subject in the sentence. In the first example, the subject is mermaids. To do this, a clause is going to be added to the sentence.

Remind the children that they already know about subordinate clauses that start with subordinating conjunctions; however, to add a clause that provides more information about the subject, a different type of subordinate clause needs to be used.

Return to the strip of card that has the first sentence written on it:

Mermaids live at the bottom of the sea.

Explain that the subordinate clause that is going to be added is neither at the beginning nor the middle of the sentence, but it is going to be placed somewhere inside it.

Ask the children if they can work out where the clause may be inserted. If no one knows, use some scissors and cut the strip between *Mermaids* and the rest of the clause.

Take another strip and write on it:

who are beautiful fish-like creatures

Place this strip between the two parts of the original sentence. It should now read:

Mermaids, who are beautiful fish-like creatures, live at the bottom of the sea.

Explain that you have now created a multi-clause sentence: the main clause has been split and the subordinate clause has been embedded within it. This type of clause is known as a relative clause because it starts with a relative pronoun – in this instance, *who*. *Who* is used because the relative clause is referring to a person or persons. As the clause is embedded within the main clause, you will need to explain that a comma is needed at each end of the new clause in order to separate it from the main clause.

With this sentence, a relative clause has been embedded between the subject and the verb; however, it is also possible to add a relative clause at the end of the sentence, thus providing more information about the bottom of the sea, which is the object in the sentence. The clause added to the end of the sentences should start with *which* or *that* because it is providing information about a thing rather than a person. It could also start with *where*.

Ask the children to think about how they might complete the new relative clause:
Mermaids live at the bottom of the sea *which* . . .
Possible answers could include:

- *Mermaids live at the bottom of the sea **which** is home to numerous sea creatures.*
- *Mermaids live at the bottom of the sea **which** is clear and warm.*
- *Mermaids live at the bottom of the sea **which** is home to beautiful coral reefs.*
- *Mermaids live at the bottom of the sea **where** all types of amazing creatures can be found.*

Ask the children to add some relative clauses to the second sentence:

Ogres prefer to live in swamps.

Ask them to embed a relative clause that will start with *who*. This clause will refer to ogres.

Then ask them to add a clause to the end of the sentence starting with either *that* or *which*. This clause will refer to swamps.

Possible clauses could be:

Ogres, **who** *are often solitary creatures, prefer to live in swamps.*
Ogres prefer to live in swamps **which** *are smelly and dirty.*

Stress to the children that relative clauses help to make writing more fluent and provide more information about either the subject or the object.

Finish this session by asking the children to explain how they have created their relative clauses.

LITTLE AND OFTEN ACTIVITIES

RELATIVE FACTS

Can the children match up the following to make five sentences, each containing an embedded clause? This could be a colour-coding activity, or all the various parts of the sentences could be cut up on cards for the children to sort.

A more active way of organising this activity is to have all the following written on large pieces of card. Each child has one and has the task of moving around to make a trio formed of two parts of the main clause and the relative clause. Of course, it will have to make sense.

The largest egg in the world,	which is the peregrine falcon,	is a sparrow-sized bird with a brown body.
The fastest flying bird,	which is the most common bird in the wild,	is up to 60cm long.
The Belcher's sea snake,	who is the founder of Microsoft,	can fly up to 105 miles per hour.
The red-billed quelea,	which is laid by the whale shark,	is found in the seas off South East Asia and Northern Australia.
Bill Gates,	which is the most venomous snake in the world,	was named the richest person in the world in 2015.

Once the children have agreed on all the sentences, ask them to read them aloud to check that they do make sense.

ADDING RELATIVE CLAUSES

Provide several single-clause sentences and encourage the children to add relative clauses either by embedding them or adding them to the end of the sentence. Sometimes they may be able to add two to the same sentence.

The following sentences are all based on the character Harry Potter, but obviously, they could be about anything or anyone. It is useful to relate them to something that the children know or are working on.

- *Harry Potter is a young wizard.*
- *Harry goes to Hogwarts School.*
- *Ron Weasley is Harry's best friend.*
- *Professor Dumbledore is the headmaster of Hogwarts School.*
- *Hedwig is Harry's pet.*
- *Hagrid always tries to make sure that Harry is safe.*

If the children do not know the Harry Potter books well, they could always make up some facts. Alternatively, provide the same task based on characters in a book that they do know.

Once the children have completed their sentences by adding relative clauses, ask them to look at the clauses that have been embedded. The relative clauses should all start with a relative pronoun, mainly *who*. Ask them to think whether they have written any clause where the relative pronoun could be omitted so that it is just implied – for example:

Harry, who is James and Lily Potter's son, goes to Hogwarts School.

This could become:

Harry, James and Lily Potter's son, goes to Hogwarts School.

The second sentence with the implied relative pronoun sounds smoother than the first.

OMITTING THE RELATIVE PRONOUNS

Share several sentences, which all contain relative pronouns, with the children. Ask them to decide whether it is possible to remove the relative pronoun so that it is only implied, but ensure that the sentence still makes sense. For each sentence, they will need to identify the relative pronoun and then check whether it needs to be there. This could be a listening activity with children either showing thumbs up or down to indicate whether the pronoun could be omitted. The following are possible sentences that could be used:

- *Where's the book that I lent you yesterday?*
- *I like the girl who has just joined our class.*
- *The flowers that Auntie Jan gave us are lovely.*
- *Josie is wearing a top that is covered in dirty marks.*
- *Mrs Parker, who has five sons, lives in a very big house.*
- *There was panic everywhere in the school when the fire alarm was set off accidentally.*
- *The park, which is at the end of our street, has a brilliant climbing frame.*

MIX AND MATCH CLAUSES

Organise the children to work in groups. Provide each group with a list of main and relative clauses, some cardboard strips and a pair of scissors. The children need to write

(Continued)

(Continued)

each clause on a separate strip, deciding whether each one is a main clause or a relative clause. They then need to pair these up in order to create multi-clause sentences. If the relative clause is to be embedded, they need to cut the main clause in the correct place. If the clause is to be added at the end, they do not need to cut anything. Finally, if they think that the relative pronoun in the embedded clause could be implied, they should cut that clause to remove it. Their final task is to add the punctuation: the embedded clause will need a comma at both ends, whereas the clauses at the end of the sentences will not need a comma. They must, of course, ensure that the final sentence starts with a capital letter and ends with a full stop.

You could use the clauses below or add some more of your own.

I am good friends with John	who moved in last week
my friend always makes me laugh	who were pumping water as fast as possible
next summer I am going to France	who were wearing exquisite costumes
my dad's car is falling to pieces	who lives next door
the rescuers managed to save the trapped diver	that takes exercise seriously
the dancers performed well in the show	where my best friend lives
my next-door neighbours are very noisy	which is very old
he is a man	who tells really bad jokes

Finding examples in reading

Non-fiction

Relative clauses are likely to be found in both fiction and factual writing. Many entries in the DK *Why? Encyclopedia* (2014) provide good examples of how relative clauses can be used to link information succinctly in factual writing. Share the following examples and ask the children to locate the relative clauses. They could also look at some of the information books in the classroom or the library in order to locate their own examples.

The following has one relative clause with an implied relative pronoun:

How many stars are there?

*Our galaxy, **called the Milky Way**, has hundreds of billions of stars. There are trillions more galaxies in the Universe, each containing countless stars. From the Earth, the Milky Way looks like a band of light in the night sky. If you could fly above our galaxy, it would look like a glittering wheel.*

(DK *Why? Encyclopedia*, 2014, p6)

This passage has two relative clauses:

Why does it rain?

*The clouds in the sky are made up of tiny water droplets **which rise into the air when the Sun heats the sea**. The droplets get larger and heavier, then fall to the* *ground as rain. This water runs into rivers **which flow from the land back to the sea**. This never-ending journey is called the water cycle.*

(DK *Why? Encyclopedia*, 2014, p36)

Fiction

It is also interesting to notice how relative clauses work in fiction, often providing additional information about characters. The following extract from *A Series of Unfortunate Events: The Bad Beginning* by Lemony Snickett contains three relative clauses that tell the reader more about the character, Mr Poe: one starts with the relative pronoun *which*, and the other two, which come together, start with *when* and *where*.

> *Mr Poe took off his top hat, **which had made his head look large and square in the fog**, and stood for a moment coughing loudly into a white handkerchief. Violet and Klaus moved forward to shake his hand and say how do you do.*
>
> *"How do you do?" said Violet.*
>
> *"How do you do?" said Klaus.*
>
> *"Odo yow!" said Sunny.*
>
> *"Fine, thank you," said Mr Poe, but he looked very sad. For a few seconds nobody said anything, and the children wondered what Mr Poe was doing there at Briny Beach, **when he should have been at the bank in the city, where he worked**. He was not dressed for the beach.*

(Lemony Snicket, *A Series of Unfortunate Events: The Bad Beginning*, 1999, pp6–7)

The three relative clauses in this short extract demonstrate well how relative pronouns are used to create relative clauses and how these clauses help to add additional information in a fluent and coherent way. One is an embedded clause whereas the other two are added to the end of a main clause.

Applying in writing

Character description

Ask the children to think of a character they know well either from a book or from the screen. Challenge them to write down everything they know about the character in note form. Once they have done this, tell them to look at all the facts they have written and ask them to cluster these facts into groups.

They now need to write five multi-clause sentences containing relative clauses about the character. Once this is done, ask them to write a character description that contains some of the sentences that they have just created.

Point out that not all the sentences should contain a relative clause and that there needs to be a balance of different types of sentences.

Information writing

This can either be about a real creature or about one that the children have made up.

If the children are writing about a real creature, the task can involve developing research skills.

Ask the children to make notes about their creature and then work in the ways described for the character description. This will be more formal writing, so the children will need to adopt a more formal tone.

TERMINOLOGY

- clause
- main clause
- subordinate clause
- relative clause
- embedded clause

- pronoun
- relative pronoun
- subject
- object
- comma

Reference

Department for Education (DfE) (2014) *National Curriculum in England: framework for key stages 1 to 4*. London: Department for Education.

CHAPTER 3.8

YEARS 5 AND 6 PUNCTUATION

Vocabulary, grammar and punctuation statutory requirements

Pupils should be taught to indicate grammatical and other features by:

- using commas to clarify meaning and avoid ambiguity in writing;
- using hyphens to avoid ambiguity;
- using brackets, dashes or commas to indicate parenthesis;
- using semi-colons, colons or dashes to mark boundaries between independent clauses;
- using a colon to introduce a list;
- punctuating bullet points consistently.

I believe that a well-chosen piece of punctuation is as good as a well-chosen word. It is important that children understand this and to realise that, as writers, they can choose punctuation for effect and to enhance meaning in the same way that they choose words.

Punctuation is often the poor relation in the world of writing with more focus being given to ideas and words. If writing is not punctuated correctly, though, it will not make sense to the reader. Therefore, in order to be able to understand and use punctuation effectively in writing, children need to be able to hear it in spoken language and to pay attention to it in their own reading.

Essential knowledge

Using commas to clarify meaning and avoid ambiguity in writing

A comma is a punctuation mark used to help the reader by separating parts of a sentence. It sometimes corresponds to a pause in speech and is used for a variety of reasons:

To separate items in a list (but not usually before and):

My favourite sports are football, tennis, swimming and gymnastics.
I got home, had a bath and went to bed.

To mark off extra information (parenthesis):

Jill, my boss, is 28 years old.

After a subordinate clause which begins a sentence:

Although it was cold, we didn't wear our coats.

With a fronted adverbial:

Anyway, In the end, After a while

Children will have already learned about using commas in a list in Year 2 and about placing commas before fronted adverbials (including subordinate clauses) in Year 4.

New learning in Years 5 and 6 will focus on using commas to separate relative clauses and parenthesis. However, the key aspect to focus on is how commas can clarify meaning and avoid ambiguity.

LITTLE AND OFTEN ACTIVITY

Provide the children with some sentences where the comma is missing. Ask them to insert a comma in order to clarify the meaning:

Charlie James and Ahmed play on the same football team.

Ask the children to use commas to show whether there are two or three children in the same team:

Charlie James and Ahmed play on the same team. (two children)
Charlie, James and Ahmed play on the same team. (three children)

Show the following sentences and ask the children to explain the difference in meaning between the two:

Elephants, that live in Africa, have big ears.
Elephants that live in Africa have big ears.

The first sentence is saying that all elephants have big ears. The parenthesis implies that elephants only live in Africa.

The second sentence suggests that only elephants that live in Africa have big ears; it also suggests that elephants may live in other parts of the word too.

Show the children the following sentence and ask what Miriam likes doing:

Miriam likes cooking her family and her pets.

Because there is a comma missing, this sentence makes Miriam sound quite alarming with a tendency to eat humans. Ask the children to add a comma in order to make Miriam sound far more friendly:

Miriam likes cooking, her family and her pets.

USING HYPHENS TO AVOID AMBIGUITY

Tell the children that the main purpose of a hyphen is to glue words together. It should never be mistaken for a dash, which is longer and has an entirely different purpose. They often occur when creating new adjectives – for example:

- *a walk-in wardrobe*
- *a top-quality buffet*
- *a well-trodden path*

Can the children use these hyphenated words in sentences?

Ask the children to keep an eye out for hyphenated words when they are reading and to make a class collection of these.

AVOIDING AMBIGUITY: SPOT THE DIFFERENCE

Ask the children to explain the difference between the following sets of words and phrases:

re-sent	resent
in-form	inform
re-form	reform
two-year old children	two year old children
little-known fact	little known fact
re-sign	resign
re-creation	recreation
re-cover	recover

(Continued)

(Continued)

AVOIDING AMBIGUITY: NEWSPAPER HEADLINES

Share some possible newspaper headlines with the children.
Ask them to work out the difference between:

Man eating shark

and

Man-eating shark.

In the first headline a man is eating a shark, whereas the second headline is reporting on a shark that eats men/humans.
Ask them to predict what the possible news story might focus on.
Try some other ambiguous headlines:

Ancient history teacher visits Roman ruins!

or

Ancient-history teacher visits Roman ruins!

Mother-to-be in serious accident!

or

Mother to be in serious accident!

And what is for sale in this advert?

Three year old puppies for sale!

The seller could be advertising that there are three puppies that are all one year old; on the other hand, he may not have specified the number of puppies but they are all three years old.

Essential knowledge

Using brackets, dashes or commas to indicate parenthesis

A parenthesis is a word or phrase inserted into a sentence to explain or elaborate. It may be placed inside brackets or between dashes or commas:

- *Sam and Emma (Tom's oldest children) are coming to visit him next weekend.*
- *Margaret is generally happy — she sings in the mornings! — but sometimes she becomes fed up with her job.*
- *Sarah is, I believe, the best musician in the class.*

You should be able to remove the information inside the commas, dashes or brackets and the sentence will still make sense.

The term 'parenthesis' can also refer to the brackets themselves. When creating parenthesis, writers can choose whether to use commas, dashes or brackets. They may base their choice on the degree of formality in the writing. Dashes are least formal, so likely to be used in a chatty email or a jokey diary entry. Commas are next in degrees of formality. Most formal are brackets and are likely to be used in a more formal piece of writing such as a respectful letter or when providing factual information in an encyclopedia.

Learning about punctuating parenthesis fits well with work on relative clauses.

LITTLE AND OFTEN ACTIVITIES

CREATING PARENTHESIS

Display the following sentences on the board:

Mr Lewis always sets very difficult homework.

Mr Lewis, the strictest teacher in the school, always sets very difficult homework.

Ask the children what they notice about the sentences.

The second sentence has some additional information which has been demarcated with commas. If you took the words between the commas away, the two sentences would be the same. When you add extra information – for interest or clarification – this is called parenthesis.

Provide some more sentences on the board – for example:

Mrs Ahmed strolled to the local park.

Daniel was always the first to complete his homework.

Mrs Turnbull glared at the class.

Ask the children, either on mini whiteboards or in writing books or journals, to think of something extra to tell the reader about Mrs Ahmed and to add it in to the sentence. They need to decide where the information is going and to punctuate correctly with commas. The information should be added after the subject which, in this case, is Mrs Ahmed. They should then do the same with Daniel and Mrs Turnbull.

The sentences provided are just examples; it would be useful to provide sentences that fit in with the work they are doing.

BRACKETS, DASHES OR COMMAS?

Provide different forms of writing and get the children to agree which punctuation marks they will use for parenthesis depending on the level of formality.

- *Early that morning, George and Anton tiptoed down the stairs and out through the back door.* (moderately formal – commas)
- *Hi Bella. Can't wait to tell you about the fun we had at the party. The pizzas were amazing and the music was great!* (least formal – dashes)

(Continued)

(Continued)

Henry VIII had six wives. (most formal – brackets)

Having identified the different types of writing, ask the children to work in pairs to suggest some parenthesis for each sentence and to insert and punctuate it correctly.

ADDING IN THE PUNCTUATION

Provide several sentences that include parenthesis but are not correctly punctuated. Ask the children to decide where the punctuation should be placed and to choose whether to use dashes, brackets or commas. Ask them to explain their choices.

Mr Khan a local businessman donated one thousand pounds to the school fund.
Alice Granger school cook for over thirty years retired last Friday.
Tenerife the largest Canary Island is a popular holiday destination.
Liam Mortimer the local postman saved a cat that was trapped in a post-box.
Daisy my best friend always makes me laugh.

MIX AND MATCH

Provide the children with a copy of the following sentences and the possible parenthesis on strips of paper. Ask them to decide which piece of parenthesis could be inserted in each sentence. Once they have decided, ask the children to cut the sentence in the correct place and insert the parenthesis. Finally, they should decide whether they will use dashes, commas or brackets to correctly punctuate the sentences.

Mr Davies was quick to come to the rescue of his son.	aged 23
The IOC decides where the Olympic Games will be held.	a supporter for over thirty years
Miss Denny walked nervously into the classroom.	a six-week-old kitten
Misty had to be rescued from under the old, dusty floorboards.	my next-door neighbour for many years
Asif Khan was defeated in the second round.	a huge sci-fi fan
Our class visited Alton Towers last week.	Tom's father
Dorothy Howe moved into a new flat last week.	chair of the school council
Callum Brown never misses Manchester City's home matches.	last year's champion
Maya Williams claimed to have seen a strange object flying across the sky.	International Olympic Committee
Annie Warren announced the winner of the writing competition.	6B

Finding examples in reading

Find the parenthesis: ask children to find a page from a non-fiction text. Can they locate any parenthesis? Which punctuation marks have been used? Make a class tally. Which type of punctuation for parenthesis have they found the most of?

Essential knowledge

Using semi-colons, colons or dashes to mark boundaries between independent clauses

Semi-colons, dashes and colons can be used to separate two main (independent) clauses in a sentence. Semi-colons and dashes are used to show a connection between two clauses, whereas colons are specifically used to show that the second clause is explaining or expanding on the first.

I liked the book: it was enjoyable to read.

This could also have been written as two separate sentences:

I liked the book. It was enjoyable to read.

Or joined with a conjunction:

I liked the book because it was enjoyable to read.

However, where the two clauses are closely related in meaning (as in the above example), a writer may prefer to use a colon rather than two separate sentences. Semi-colons and dashes can be used more widely than colons. They indicate to the reader that both clauses have some connection. Dashes tend to be more informal than semi-colons, though, and you are unlikely to find them in formal writing:

The door creaked open; there was no one to be seen.
James was given a new football – he played with it as soon as he arrived home.
Alice was exhausted – she had stayed up late to complete her maths homework.

It is important to note that colons, semi-colons and dashes can only be used with independent clauses; it is incorrect to use them where there is subordination.

Semi-colons in formal writing: balanced arguments

Semi-colons are useful when writing balanced arguments as they are useful in indicating a contrast between opposing ideas.
  Show two sentences on the board showing two different sides of an argument:

Many children think they should be allowed to stay up late at the weekends. Most parents believe that it is still important that young people get enough sleep.

Explain to the children that when there are two related clauses – in this case providing a contrast – they can be punctuated with a semi-colon instead of a full stop:

Many children think they should be allowed to stay up late at the weekends; most parents believe that it is still important that young people get enough sleep.

Ask whether the children can think of any contrasting word or phrase that they could put straight after the semi-colon. The most likely word is 'however':

Many children think they should be allowed to stay up late at the weekends; however, most parents believe that it is still important that young people get enough sleep.

Point out the comma after 'however' – it is there to tell the reader to take a slight pause.
  Show some more sentences on the board. Ask the children to add a contrasting clause and use a semi-colon to demonstrate that they are connected. Get them to use mini-whiteboards

for the first one so that they can share and explain their ideas. Check that they have changed the full stop to a semi-colon before adding the contrasting clause.

Most parents believe that homework is important.
Many people think that driving cars harm the environment.
Some people claim that eating too much meat is bad for you.
Teachers think that grammar and punctuation are fascinating.
Many people think that all criminals should be sent to prison.

Correct, incorrect or not needed?

Share any of the sentences listed below. Each sentence has a semi-colon placed within it. Ask the children to decide whether the semi-colon is in the correct position, in the incorrect position or not needed at all. Ask them to explain their reasons.

Amelia sat down and turned on; the television her favourite reality show was about to start. (incorrect position)
Although it was very warm; Billy went out wearing a thick jumper. (not needed because the first clause is subordinate)
I love going to the high street; and buying lots of clothes. (not needed because the sentences are linked with 'and')
Mum sat down with a cup of tea; it was the first time she had stopped all day. (correct)
Mrs Davies surveyed her class sternly; waiting for the culprit to own up. (not needed)
Reluctantly, Natalie pushed the door ajar; she was wondering what she would find behind it. (correct)
Sophie walked towards the post box; clutching the envelope tightly would hers be the winning entry? (incorrect position)
Lily was sad to say goodbye to Mrs Hopkins; she had always been a good neighbour. (correct)
Dad was extremely worried; because William was late home from the football match. (not needed as the two clauses are linked by 'because')

The corrected sentences are listed below:

Amelia sat down and turned on the television; her favourite reality show was about to start.
Although it was very warm, Billy went out wearing a thick jumper.
I love going to the high street and buying lots of clothes.
Mum sat down with a cup of tea; it was the first time she had stopped all day.
Mrs Davies surveyed her class sternly waiting for the culprit to own up.
Reluctantly, Natalie pushed the door ajar; she was wondering what she would find behind it.
Sophie walked towards the post box clutching the envelope tightly; would hers be the winning entry?
Lily was sad to say goodbye to Mrs Hopkins; she had always been a good neighbour.
Dad was extremely worried because William was late home from the football match.

Colon or semi-colon?

Sometimes it is difficult to work out whether a colon or a semi-colon should be used to join two independent clauses. Ask the children to work out whether the second clause explains or illustrates the first clause. If it does, they should use a colon; if it does not, then the correct choice is a semi-colon.

The children took off their boots and left them by the front door. Aunt Mary was very fussy about her new carpets.

A colon would be correct here as the second clause is explaining why the children took their boots off.

Sally's birthday is in September. Alan's is in December.

A semi-colon is correct here because the second clause does not explain the first; it shows a difference.

Ask the children to work out these:

Roald Dahl wrote numerous children's books. He also wrote some books for adults. (semi-colon)
Mrs Evans was late for her meeting at school. The train was late. (colon)

You can also provide the children with some clauses that end either with a semi-colon or a colon. Ask them to write the next clause remembering that if there is a colon, the next clause must expand or illustrate the one that is already there. If there is a semi-colon, this has to show a connection in a different way.

Mrs Lewis stepped outside into a huge puddle;
Tom gasped as he opened the door:
The poor man burst into tears:
Our dogs raced around the field:

With the clauses below, ask the children to write the preceding clause:

: there was no time to waste.
; Tom was always late with his.
: the tide was coming in rapidly.
; it was empty.

Finding examples in reading

Dashes

Michael Morpurgo tends to include more dashes in his writing than many other writers, so it is worth looking as how he uses them and the impact they have. Below are some examples from *Private Peaceful*.

> *She moved in the next week to look after us. She wasn't our grandmother at all, not really – both our grandmothers were dead.*
>
> *Big Joe loved the mice – he'd even put out food for them.*
>
> *Both Charlie and Molly had found work up in the Big House – almost everyone in the village worked up there or on the estate.*

(Michael Morpurgo, *Private Peaceful*, 2003)

Ask the children to locate more examples in the book where dashes have been used to mark the clauses. As they start to see how they are used, the children could start to use them in their own writing.

Ask them to look in other books by other authors to see whether they can find more examples of dashes being used – either to create parenthesis or to link two independent clauses.

Using a colon to introduce a list

Colons are often used to introduce lists, particularly if you want the reader to pause before moving on to the lists. A 'colon pause' is slightly longer than one you would take after a semi-colon, but is not as long as one that you would take with a full stop. The pause created by the colon draws attention to what is coming next in the list. This is particularly useful when the list is long or contains complicated items; however, if the list is short and contains relatively simple items, you may not need to use a colon.

A guiding rule to help determine whether to use a colon to introduce a list is to look at the words that precede the list: if they form a clause that can stand on its own, you should use a colon, but if they do not, one should not be used – for example:

The spell contained some unusual ingredients: bats' wings, frogs' legs, a human eye and some snake venom. (correct use of the colon)

The spell contained bats' wings, frogs' legs, a human eye and some snake venom. (no need to use a colon)

Provide the children with some sentences containing lists and ask them to decide whether a colon is needed in each one.

Colons have been placed in all the examples below, but are they all correct? Ask the children to decide whether the colon is needed and to explain their reasons.

During the party, the children will play: Blind Man's Bluff, Musical Chairs, Hide and Seek, and Pass the Parcel. (incorrect)
I need to buy these ingredients to make the cake: caster sugar, butter, eggs and flour. (correct)
We are going to invite: Tom, Samantha, Leon, Mandip and Charlie. (incorrect)

There is going to be some fabulous entertainment: clowns, magicians and street dancing. (correct)
We need to: book the village hall, send invitations and provide party bags for all the guests. (incorrect)

Remember that the colon is only needed when the list is preceded by an independent clause that stands on its own. Therefore, only the second and fourth examples actually require a colon.

Ask the children to look at the sentences where the colon is used incorrectly and challenge them to rewrite the sentences so that it is necessary to use a colon. For example:

We are going to invite all our best friends: Tom, Samantha, Leon, Mandip and Charlie.

Punctuating bullet points consistently

There are different ways that bullet points can be punctuated.

In a list where each bulleted point is a complete sentence, a full stop is used:

Mrs Adams made three suggestions to help her class improve their stories:

* *Writing should be clear and legible.*

- *Words need to be chosen with care.*

- *Every sentence must be punctuated correctly.*

In a list which is a continuous sentence, semi-colons should be used along with a full stop after the last bullet point. Also, each bullet point should start with a lower-case letter:

When tidying your bedroom, please remember to:

- *bring the dirty plates and glasses downstairs;*

- *hang up clean clothes and put dirty ones in the laundry basket; and*

- *make sure all the surfaces are clear.*

A list of very short points may not need any punctuation:

We need:

- *paper*

- *scissors*

- *straws*

- *sticky tape*

The important point is to make sure that whichever way the bullet points are being punctuated, it is consistent throughout.

Choosing the correct punctuation

Once the children have learned the full range of punctuation that is covered in Key Stage 2, it is useful to provide challenges where they must decide which is the most appropriate punctuation. The following Little and Often activities help to do this.

LITTLE AND OFTEN ACTIVITIES

RUNAROUND

This is a moving around activity and would work best in the hall or out in the playground. The idea is to pick any three punctuation marks and have them displayed. For example, you could have a semi-colon, a comma and some brackets. The children need to listen carefully as you say a sentence clearly. They then need to decide which punctuation is needed within the sentence and go in front of the corresponding punctuation mark. Once they have all made their decision, they are allowed five seconds to change their mind. (This is a little like the children's TV show *Runaround* which ran in the late seventies and early eighties.)

When all the children have finalised their decisions, ask them where in the sentence the punctuation should go and why.

(Continued)

(Continued)

Here are some example sentences that you could use, but you can also make up some more.

It was a beautiful sunny day; Joe decided to do some gardening.

The semi-colon is needed here to show that the two clauses are linked.

Dr Magnus (a highly skilled neurosurgeon) performed the operation.

The brackets are used here because there is some parenthesis in the sentence.

Mutley was in big trouble; he had trailed mud all through the house.

The semi-colon is used to show that the two independent clauses are related.

When it was time for a bath, Lily hid under the table.

The comma is used here to separate the subordinate clause from the main clause.

Reluctantly, Shona started to do her maths homework.

The comma is used to separate the fronted adverbial from the rest of the sentence.

The blue whale (the world's largest mammal) is often found in the Pacific Ocean off the California coast.

The brackets are used because the sentence contains parenthesis.

I SPY WITH MY LITTLE EYE ... /I HEAR WITH MY LITTLE EAR ...

These are either reading or listening activities. Find a short text which has a variety of punctuation within it. Get the children to read the text and to record the different types of punctuation used. As a follow-up, ask them to explain why the punctuation has been used.

However, it is also helpful for children to be able to hear punctuation, so you could also read the text out loud. Provide punctuation fans, cards with the punctuation displayed or mini white boards for the children to show their answers. Every time they think they hear some punctuation, ask them to show which mark they think has been used. Most importantly, ask the children to explain their answers so that they demonstrate that they understand how each one works.

A different way of running this game with a small group is to provide each child with a different punctuation mark. Again, read the text out loud, but only the child who has the correct punctuation shows it. (Of course, there may be a discussion at times, as often it may be possible to choose different punctuation for effect.)

The children could tally their results which will give a good indication of which aspects of punctuation are most commonly used.

DECISIONS, DECISIONS

This activity focuses on the use of commas, semi-colons and colons; however, it could work when thinking about any punctuation that is taught at Key Stage 2. Show the children several sentences that have some of the above punctuation missing and challenge the children to work out what it is.

Ideally, they could use punctuation fans or have three different cards that show a comma, a colon and a semi-colon. Alternatively, they could devise hand signs that illustrate these three punctuation marks.

This is a three-part challenge. First, show each sentence separately and ask the children to show you what punctuation is missing. It is useful for them all to show you what they think at the same time. Start with just one missing piece, but you could move on to having several pieces missing to create more of a challenge.

After the missing punctuation has been correctly identified, ask one child to tell you where it should be placed.

The final part of the challenge is to ask someone to explain why it should be included in the sentence.

Below are some examples, but you can easily create your own.

I think I have remembered everything tickets, passports, snacks, maps and magazines.
(a colon after **everything** to introduce a list)
All my tools were stolen a hammer, saw, screwdriver and wire cutters.
(a colon after **stolen** to introduce a list)
Ed strolled nonchalantly towards the closed door he raised his hand ready to knock.
(a semi-colon after **door** to show two related independent clauses)
When I went to Sri Lanka I saw elephants bathing in a water hole blue whales swimming in the Indian Ocean and a leopard strolling through Yala National Park.
(a comma after **Sri Lanka** to separate the subordinate clause from the main clause, and semi-colons after **hole** and **Ocean** to separate items in a list)
Dan hesitated before opening the door he could hear a strange noise coming from inside.
(a colon after **door** to show that the second independent clause is explaining the first)
Lions roamed freely across the plains it was an awesome sight.
(a semi-colon after **plains** to show that the two independent clauses are related)
There was an enormous puddle outside the front door it had been raining heavily all through the night.
(a colon after **door** to show that the second independent clause explains the first)

TERMINOLOGY

colon	brackets
semi-colon	comma
dash	clause
hyphen	ambiguity
parenthesis	bullet points

PART 4

YOU'VE TAUGHT IT BUT HAVE THEY LEARNT IT?

CHAPTER 4.1
ASSESSMENT

As is evident from the previous parts, the statutory requirements for grammar and punctuation at Key Stage 2 may appear complicated; however, with systematic and good quality teaching, they do not have to be.

The good news is that there is plenty of time to teach everything – four years, in fact. However, this is dependent on each year group playing its part in ensuring that children have been taught, and therefore have learnt, what they need. To make sure that this is the case, teachers need to keep checking and assessing what has been learnt and, more importantly, what has been understood.

The American psychiatrist, William Glasser, said this about learning:

We learn:

10% of what we read

20% of what we hear

30% of what we see

50% of what we both see and hear

70% of what is discussed

80% of what we experience personally

95% of what we teach someone else.

If this is the case, which I believe it is, there are some major implications here about how grammar and punctuation are taught to ensure that it is really learnt and understood. This is why so many of the activities described in this book require children to talk and to explain their thinking.

In addition to Glasser, Jerome Bruner, an American psychologist, talked about the spiral curriculum. It is an approach to education that introduces key concepts to students at a young age and covers these concepts repeatedly, with increasing degrees of complexity.

This is why there are numerous Little and Often activities in this book as they provide the opportunity for children to visit the statutory requirements repeatedly, thus developing deeper understanding and confidence.

It is also the reason that links are always made to what has been taught in previous years and what is yet to be taught.

Having taught everything that needs to be covered, in the right order and in the correct year, and revisited statutory requirements many times, teachers still need to make sure that what has been taught has actually been learnt. This is where assessment comes in.

There are many ways to assess the learning and understanding in grammar and punctuation: the next few pages will explore some ways of doing so.

The most powerful assessment is the everyday formative assessment that occurs in the classroom. If you have just spent ten minutes explaining and demonstrating the present perfect, but you are facing a sea of blank faces, you know that this concept is not understood and that there is much more work to be done. Equally, children sometimes grasp a new concept more rapidly than anticipated, which is a good indication to move the learning on. This should lead to an immediate deviation from what has been planned and will also impact on the following days' lessons.

Making discussion an integral part of all grammar and punctuation teaching helps this. Thinking about William Glasser's theory, if the children cannot explain something, they have not really understood it.

Alongside everyday Assessment for Learning, though, there needs to be times when the learning is assessed in a more formal way that can be used diagnostically to inform future planning.

Assessment activities

I do not believe that there is any need to make children sit endless tests in order to assess what they know, particularly as they near the statutory assessment tasks at the end of Key Stage 2. I do think they should have some experience of sitting a practice test in order to gain an understanding of the breadth and style of questions asked and to learn how to manage their time. It is also useful for teachers to incorporate some of the question types into their Little and Often activities as the test date nears. However, is there any value in children sitting more than a couple of practice tests? I think not, and I do believe that there are better ways of assessing what the children understand.

Assessing understanding through reading

Every time a child reads, they are exposed to grammar and punctuation. Sometimes they will notice the grammar and use it to check their understanding, and at other times they will not. Therefore, it is often useful, through providing a short piece of text, to ask them to indicate, perhaps using a highlighter, what they understand to be there.

The short news stories on the bbc newsround website (**www.bbc.co.uk/newsround**) are extremely useful for this, although you could actually use any short extract, either fact or fiction. Probably the most useful reading extracts to assess understanding are the ones that you write yourself as these will include all the grammar and punctuation that you want the children to identify.

The following extract was found on **www.bbc.co.uk/newsround** and contains many features from the Key Stage 2 curriculum:

Dippy the diplodocus set for UK tour

One of the UK's most famous dinosaurs, Dippy the diplodocus, could be coming to a town near you.

At the beginning of the year, a campaign was launched to save Dippy, the 109-year-old diplodocus skeleton cast that has been in the Natural History Museum's entrance hall in London since 1979.

Thousands of people signed a petition to keep the dinosaur, rather than a new blue whale model, but now the museum has announced plans to send Dippy on tour around the country from early 2018.

A full list of where it will go hasn't been decided yet but the 21 metre long skeleton will need to be taken apart and re-built at each venue.

You could allow children the freedom to highlight anything that they notice. This is probably most useful in terms of assessing their understanding as it tells you what they are aware of and what they are not.

However, you could also provide a list of grammatical features and punctuation that are in the extract which they should be able to find – for example:

Expanded noun phrase	*One of the UK's most famous dinosaurs the 109-year-old diplodocus skeleton cast that has been in the Natural History Museum's entrance hall in London since 1979.*
Possessive apostrophe	*UK's*
Parenthesis (using commas)	*, Dippy the diplodocus, , rather than a new blue whale model,*
Modal verb	*could be coming, will need*
Fronted adverbial	*At the beginning of the year,*
Commas for fronted adverbials	*At the beginning of the year,*
Passive construction	*a campaign was launched*
Present perfect	*has been, the museum has announced*
Hyphens to avoid ambiguity	*the 109-year-old diplodocus, re-built*

The following extract is taken from one of the stories in *The Story Shop!* compiled by Nikki Gamble. It is the start of 'A Lighthouse Heroine' by Henry Brook.

In the mist and spray thrown up by the storm, the survivors on the rock must have thought they were seeing things. A tiny rowing boat was nudging towards them out of the gloom, with a middle-aged man waving from its prow and a young girl pulling confidently at the oars. The girl's courage and proficiency startled the sailors in the party. They weren't used to seeing a woman who was as skilled on the water as they were. At any second, the sea threatened to pick the fragile craft up and smash it onto the same rocks that had crushed their own ship. But the girl worked the oars expertly, correcting the drift and turning into the waves, to prevent the boat from capsizing.

She rowed closer, never stopping to think of the danger she was in. Her name was Grace Darling, and her daring at sea would make her one of the greatest celebrities of her time.

This extract could be suitable for Years 3 or 4 children as there are many interesting examples of grammar that is covered in the Y3/4 statutory requirements, although it does also contain modal verbs and relative clauses which would test children in Years 5 and 6.

However, younger children could look for:

Fronted adverbials marked by commas	*In the mist and spray thrown by the storm, At any second,*
Past progressive (revision from Key Stage 1)	*they were seeing things, was nudging*
Present perfect	*must have thought, that had crushed*
Prepositional phrases	*in the mist and spray, out of the gloom, with a middle-aged man, at sea*
Possessive apostrophe for singular possession (revision from Key Stage 1)	*the girl's courage*
Apostrophe for contraction (revision from Key Stage 1)	*they weren't*
Pronouns	*they, them, its, it, their, she, her*
Capital letters for names (revision from Key Stage 1)	*Grace Darling*

Each feature could be colour coded and marked in a different colour. If children are highlighting certain features, that is a good indicator that they understand them; however, features that are commonly overlooked should provide a focus for revisiting and reteaching.

Using images for assessment

An image will always provide a useful stimulus for writing and can provide the opportunity for children to write a short assessment piece in which they are able to show off their understanding and control of grammatical features and punctuation.

It is useful to start to create a collection of images that will ignite children's imaginations. These could either be teachers' own photographs or ones that are found on the internet or in books. Any image can provide a starting point for writing; however, in a collection, I would include landscapes and sea settings, boats, lighthouses, street scenes, people, animals and anything else that will excite the children. They could be photographs, cartoons and artwork. Google images is always a good place to start, but if you are looking for something a little more unusual, you could try **www.derelictplaces. co.uk** or **www.nationalgeographic.com**. Of course, there are many websites that will provide interesting images and everyone will have their favourites.

Also, consider visiting **www.literacyshed.com** for a wide and inspiring array of film clips to incite the children's imagination. There are many ideas for writing included on the website and these will all make useful starting points for Little and Often activities, as well as writing assessments. When children are writing freely, it provides a strong opportunity to see which grammatical features they include in their writing without being prompted and those they do not. If you notice that some grammatical features of writing are either missing or are not secure, this is a clear indication that there needs to be more teaching and modelling. This may mean that you need to reconsider the areas that you planned to revisit and to change your plans.

You could try providing a starting point and issue a challenge to find out what the children know and understand: ask them to try and include the following in their writing.

Sentence knowledge

When looking at any image, ask the children to write:

- *A noun, a verb and an adjective.*
- *A noun phrase.*
- *A verb chain (simple, progressive or perfect).*
- *A prepositional phrase.*
- *Two subordinate clauses starting with subordinating conjunctions.*
- *A relative clause starting with a relative pronoun (if in Y5 or Y6).*

Tense knowledge

Still using an image as a prompt, ask the children to write a description using the present tense correctly and consistently. Challenge them to use at least one progressive form and also the present perfect if appropriate.

At another time, ask them to write consistently in the past tense, ensuring that they use a wide selection of forms – *progressive, present perfect, past perfect, past perfect progressive*

Sentence bags

If you have a sentence bag (see Chapter 1.2), ask the children to write their own cut-up words, phrases and clauses in order to create a coherent sentence.

Ask the child to explain what they have done to a partner or to the whole class.

If a child can create and talk about what they have written, it demonstrates a good understanding of sentence structure.

Word classes

Provide an image.

Can the children think of an adjective and an abstract noun – for example, *mysterious silence*? Can they then swap their phrase around to make the abstract noun the adjective and the adjective the abstract noun?

- *mysterious silence* will become *silent mystery*
- *dangerous chaos will become chaotic danger*

Challenge the children to create as many pairs as possible.

Once they have created these, provide an image for them to write about and challenge them to see how many they can include in their writing.

This activity will work with other word classes as well – for example:

Write a verb and an adverb: *walk silently*

Change to an adjective and a noun: *a silent walk*

By providing an activity such as this, it is possible to determine a child's understanding of different word classes while building up a bank of phrases to use in creative writing.

Related clauses

Ask the children to write two separate single clause sentences related to an image. Then ask them to join both to create a multi-clause sentence. Depending on which year group you are working with, you may ask them to focus on subordinating conjunctions, relative pronouns or different punctuation.

Ask them to demonstrate how many ways they can join the clauses and to explain how each time they have altered the meaning.

This will assess the ability to use conjunctions, relative pronouns or colons, semi-colons and dashes.

Repetition not allowed

Ask the children to write a short paragraph based on a given image. However, they are not allowed to repeat any words in the specified word class – for example, conjunctions. Each child can start with five points, but will lose one point for each word that is repeated and gain one point for each time a new word is used. This is a good activity for working on the structural word classes (determiners, pronouns, prepositions and conjunctions) as there are fewer words to choose from in these classes.

This will assess knowledge of the variety of words in a given word class.

Fronted adverbials (Years 3 and 4)

How, when and where? For any image, ask the children to think of three sentences that each start with a fronted adverbial. One should explain where, another should explain how and the third should explain when. All three will need to be punctuated with commas.

This will assess children's wider understanding of fronted adverbials, mainly using prepositions, and also their correct use of punctuation.

Using modal verbs (Years 5 and 6)

List the nine modal verbs. Encourage the children to write a paragraph about any image using as many as they can.

could, can, will, would, shall, should, may, might, must

Adverbs to indicate degrees of possibility (Years 5 and 6)

Choose any image from your collection. Provide at least five degree adverbs. Can the children use them in a paragraph in a coherent way?

certainly, maybe, definitely, possibly, clearly, obviously, perhaps, probably

Relative pronouns and relative clauses (Years 5 and 6)

Ask the children to think of an interesting sentence about the image that you have provided.

Once they have their first sentence, can they embed a relative clause?

Then ask whether they can keep the same clause, but remove the relative pronoun to leave an implied pronoun.

Big challenge

The aim of these big challenges, as described below, is to encourage children to think actively about including the grammar that they have learnt within their writing. They will not be able to achieve the expected standard at the end of Key Stage 2 if they are not able to:

- select vocabulary and grammatical structures that reflect what the writing requires, doing this mostly appropriately (e.g. using contracted forms in dialogues in narrative; using passive verbs to affect how information is presented; using modal verbs to suggest degrees of possibility);
- use a range of devices to build cohesion (e.g. conjunctions, adverbials of time and place, pronouns, synonyms) within and across paragraphs;
- use verb tenses consistently and correctly throughout their writing;
- use the range of punctuation taught at Key Stage 2 mostly correctly (e.g. inverted commas and other punctuation to indicate direct speech).

Therefore, it is useful, throughout Key Stage 2, to provide challenges that ensure that children are thinking about all of the above. Each time they write a new piece, encourage the children to write in such a way that they can gain more points. However, they will not receive points if they do not write in a coherent manner.

Big challenge: Years 3 and 4

Ask the children to write about any image and tell them that they will be awarded points for using different aspects of grammar and punctuation. They will gain **1** point for anything from the KS1 curriculum and **2** points for:

- one example of correctly punctuated speech;
- each time a fronted adverbial is used plus a bonus point if it is punctuated correctly;
- an example of the possessive apostrophe with plural nouns;
- at least three different pronouns;
- the use of the present perfect;
- for any subordinate clause linked to a main clause;
- an expanded noun phrase with at least one adjective and a prepositional phrase.

Big challenge: Years 5 and 6

Points will be awarded as for Y3/4 and in addition **3** points will be gained for:

- at least three different modal verbs;
- a relative clause plus one bonus point if the pronoun is implied;
- at least two adverbs to indicate degrees of possibility;
- one correct example of parenthesis;
- one correct example of two clauses joined by a semi-colon or a colon;
- two examples of commas used correctly;
- hyphens to avoid ambiguity.

Award **4** points for a variety of verb forms and tenses, including the perfect tense, passive verbs and the subjunctive form.

Points can always be deducted when the inclusion of a specific feature detracts from the overall coherence of the writing or is used incorrectly.

You can, of course, create your own point system, giving added value to aspects of grammar and punctuation which children find hard.

Self-reflection

After children have written, use the plenary to ask them to assess their own writing in terms of grammatical features, – For example, ask:

- Who has used a subordinate clause?
- Who has used a semi-colon?
- Who has used a passive form of verb?
- Who has used a fronted adverbial?

If a child believes that they have used one of the above – or any other feature – ask them to share it with the rest of the class who need to be listening carefully to see if they agree. This should always include a discussion about effectiveness and the reason for using the given feature.

Teaching others

Based on William Glasser's thoughts, children learn 95 per cent of what they teach others. Therefore, asking the children to 'teach' their classmates will be an extremely useful way of assessing what they know.

The best way for children to do this is to create a poster or a presentation with the key points on it. Once these have been created, the children should talk to their classmates and 'teach' them the key points.

Posters and presentations could be based on anything in the Key Stage 2 curriculum – for example:

- *The different types of pronouns and how they work.*
- *The difference between active and passive sentences.*
- *Using perfect tenses.*
- *Explaining the uses of colons and semi-colons.*

Children could also be encouraged to devise grammar and punctuation quizzes for their classmates but, of course, they must know the answers to the questions they ask.

Using all the above ideas will help to find out how well the children have learnt what has been taught. If they can demonstrate good understanding, move the learning on. However, if the children have difficulty completing some tasks, that is an indication that more teaching is needed.

Using past test papers

Of course, there is value in Y6 children experiencing a previous test paper before the actual test that is taken in May. However, there is not much point in taking too many tests and testing for the sake of testing.

Use the tests diagnostically and identify where there is a need for revisiting or further teaching.

Look at the language of the questions with the children and point out how they are expected to know and recognise all the terminology.

Examine the different types of questions – some:

- *are multiple choice;*
- *require missing punctuation to be inserted;*
- *require lines to be drawn to connect correct answers;*
- *require the child identifying the correct response;*
- *require a written explanation;*
- *require a word or words to be inserted;*
- *require particular words to be replaced;*
- *require full sentences that are punctuated correctly;*
- *require the child to identify a word class.*

As you can see, there are many variations on the way that a question may be asked. Children do need experience of being asked questions in these different ways so that they come to understand what is expected of them. Teachers should try to incorporate different ways of asking questions into their everyday Little and Often activities.

As the children move through Key Stage 2, make sure that there are regular opportunities to assess all previous learning and not just that which is current. Revisiting will help them master new learning.

Remember that the Key Stage 2 Grammar, Punctuation and Spelling test is a test of the entire Key Stage 2 curriculum and also tests Key Stage 1 knowledge and understanding too.

Strategies to support children who need to catch up

Although we would all hope that our assessments will indicate that the children are doing well and understanding the grammar concepts that have been taught, this may not always be the case. There will be some children who do find some aspects of grammar difficult, so assessment should also be used to identify where the gaps are so that these can be addressed in a systematic way.

First, work out whether there is a secure understanding of the basics (see Part 1).

If children are uncertain of the different word classes or do not know the difference between a phrase, a clause and a sentence, these need to be revisited on a daily basis. If possible, set up a small group intervention that takes place at a different time from whole-class grammar teaching. Interventions work well where they help children to catch up while still keeping up with new and current learning. Regular assessments will also ensure that you are targeting what the children really need. These small group interventions can be based on the Little and Often principles promoted in this book rather than looking for a whole host of new material.

Ask the children to identify for themselves what they find difficult and to explain what they find hard. This is useful for working out exactly what misconceptions there may be.

Use this information to amend what you may have decided to visit through the overviews suggested at the start of Parts 2 or 3. You may have planned to revisit the present perfect in term 4, but decide to revisit extending the range of conjunctions instead, because this is what is needed. Always be prepared to be flexible with your planning as the best time to address misconceptions is when they arise.

Also, use the whole curriculum to reinforce your grammar teaching as this will help all pupils to see how essential grammar and punctuation is in all areas, and to use and apply it in a variety of contexts.

If you have a literacy or grammar working wall, make sure that clear explanations and strong examples are provided for the aspects that some children are finding the most difficult. These should be referred to regularly and pupils encouraged to develop the habit of looking at these for guidance.

Most of all, though, encourage the children to keep trying, keep practising and keep asking questions, and remember to celebrate what they do know and can do.

GLOSSARY

It is not only important that children learn and use the grammar and punctuation that is identified in the National Curriculum, they need to have a grasp of the correct terminology in order to discuss it. At every moment, insist that children use the correct terminology that is appropriate for their phase and for their previous learning.

Although terminology is discussed throughout this book, the list below provides an overview in one place.

active	An active sentence is formed when the subject performs an action.
adjective	A word that provides more information about a noun. Adjectives are often used to help form expanded noun phrases.
adverb	A word that provides more information about a verb. It helps to explain how, when or where something has happened.
adverbial phrase	A group of words that tell the reader when, where or how something happened.
ambiguity	When something can be interpreted in more than one way.
apostrophe	This is a small punctuation mark which is used to show where letters have been omitted when contractions have been formed, or to show possession.
auxiliary verb	These verbs are used with other verbs and add extra meaning. They also help to form different types of verbs such as perfect and progressive.

bracket	Punctuation used to show parenthesis.
capital letter	This is used to mark the start of a new sentence or to indicate a proper noun such as the name of a person or place.
clause	A clause is a part of a sentence or it can be a complete sentence. It has to contain a subject and a verb. There are single-clause sentences and multi clause sentences. Multi-clause sentences can comprise two co-ordinating clauses or a main clause with one or more subordinate clauses.
cohesion	This is where the grammatical aspects in a text work together.
colon	This punctuation mark is used to introduce lists or direct speech. It is also used to connect two independent clauses where the second clause illustrates or explains the first.
comma	A small punctuation mark used to tell the reader to make a slight pause when reading. Commas can separate items in a list, create parenthesis or indicate the end of a subordinate clause or fronted adverbial.
command	A sentence that tells the reader to do something.
conjunction	A word that joins other words, phrases or clauses within a sentence. Conjunctions can either be co-ordinating or subordinating.
dash	A punctuation mark to show a connection between two independent clauses. It is less formal than a colon, semi-colon or brackets.
determiner	The word that precedes a noun to determine which noun is being referred to.
direct speech	This is when a speaker's words are used in a text and are punctuated by using inverted commas.
exclamation	A sentence or phrase that expresses emotion such as surprise or anger and is usually followed by an exclamation mark. Some exclamations begin with what or how but they do not need to.
exclamation mark	A punctuation mark used at the end of a sentence or phrase that shows strong emotion.
expanded noun phrase	A group of words that provide more information about a noun.
fronted adverbial	An adverbial phrase or a subordinate clause that is placed at the front of a sentence.
full stop	A small punctuation mark that indicates the end of a sentence.
hyphen	Punctuation used to join two separate words to form a new word.
inverted commas	Punctuation used to show the actual words that are spoken by someone.
main clause	A clause that is complete on its own and can form a single clause sentence.
modal verb	An auxiliary verb that indicates possibility, probability or necessity.
noun	A word that names something. There are different types of noun: common, proper, collective and abstract.
object	This is the person or thing in a sentence that is affected by an action.
parenthesis	A word or phrase that is added to a sentence to provide more information. If it is removed, the sentence would still make sense. It may be punctuated by using brackets, commas or dashes.

passive	In a passive sentence, the subject has something done to it rather than performing the action itself.
phrase	A group of words that act as one unit. There are different types of phrases such as expanded noun phrases, prepositional phrases and adverbial phrases.
preposition	A structural word that indicates time, position or direction.
progressive	A verb form that generally describes events that are in progress. An example of past progressive is *he was eating* and an example of present progressive is *he is eating*. The *-ing* suffix indicates that it is an action that is still progressing.
pronoun	A word that can be used to replace a noun or to replace an expanded noun phrase. There are many different types of pronoun; however, the ones that are covered in the National Curriculum are personal, possessive and relative.
punctuation	Punctuation is used to help the reader understand texts.
question	A sentence that asks for information.
question mark	A punctuation mark that indicates that a question has been asked.
relative clause	This is a subordinate clause that is created by using a relative pronoun such as who, that or which.
semi-colon	A punctuation mark that is used to either show a connection between two independent clauses or to separate items in a list if these are made up of phrases rather than just words. The semi-colon indicates the need for a slightly longer pause than if a comma were used.
sentence	A group of words that are connected to each other to convey meaning. A sentence can take the form of a statement, a question, an exclamation or a command. It could be single clause or multi clause.
statement	A sentence that informs the reader of something.
subject	The subject is the person or thing that a clause or a sentence is about. The subject normally performs an action unless it is in a passive construction.
subordinate clause	A subordinate clause needs to be linked to a main clause in order to be fully understood.
tense	A verb form that indicates time. Present tense indicates that something is happening now whereas past tense indicates that something has already happened. It is also possible to indicate what may or will happen in the future.
verb	A word that tells what is happening in a sentence. It may express an action, a happening, a process or a state. It will be either present or past tense.

REFERENCES

Throughout this book, I have stressed the usefulness of children being able to see the grammar conventions they have learned about in real writing. With this in mind, I have cited books where I feel that good examples are provided. However, I am sure you could pick up most children's books and find similar strong examples. There follows a list of all the books that I have referred to in each part:

Part 1: The Basics

Hughes, T and Davidson, A (1989) *The Iron Man*. London: Faber.
Rosen, M and Oxenbury, H (1993) *We're Going on a Bear Hunt*. London: Walker Books.
Yeomans, J (illustrated by Quentin Blake) (2012) *Rumbelow's Dance*. London: Anderson Press.

Part 2: Years 3 and Year 4 Statutory Requirements

Crossley-Holland, K (1998) *SHORT! A Book of Very Short Stories*. Oxford: Oxford University Press.
Dahl, R and Schindelman, J (1964) *Charlie and the Chocolate Factory*. New York: AA Knopf.
Gamble, N (2006) *The Story Shop Anthology*. London: Wayland.
Horowitz, A (2007) *Myths and Legends*. Basingstoke: Kingsfisher.
Hughes, T and Davidson, A (1989) The Iron Man. London: Faber.
Redbeard, O (2012) *Vulgar the Viking and the Rock Cake Raiders*. London: Nosy Crow.
Swindells, R (1992) *The Ice Palace*. London: Puffin Books.
Walliams, D (2017) *Grandpa's Great Escape*. London: HarperCollins.

Part 3: Years 5 and Year 6 Statutory Requirements

Ibbotson, E (2014) *The Secret of Platform 13*. London: Macmillan Children's Books.
Ibbotson, E (2014) *Journey to the River Sea*. London: Macmillan Children's Books.
Letria, JJ (2014) *If I Were a Book*. London: Chronicle Books.
Morpurgo, M (2004) *Private Peaceful*. London: Scholastic.
Paver, M (2011) *Wolf Brother*. London: Orion Children's Books.
Smith, DJ (2014) If . . . in *Why? Encyclopedia*. Basingstoke: DK Children.
Snickett, L (2012) *A Series of Unfortunate Events: The Bad Beginning*. London: Egmont.
Viorst, J (1984) *If I were in Charge of the World (and Other Worries)*. London: Athenaeum Books.
Wilkinson, A (2008) *If I were a Sheep*. London: Jellycat Books.

Part 4: Assessment

Gamble, N (2006) *The Story Shop Anthology*. London: Wayland.

INDEX

Page numbers in **bold** denote glossary entries

abstract nouns
    activities 93–4
    examples of 4
    nominalisation 95–6
active **163**
active/passive verbs
    activities 102–4
    essential knowledge 99
    National Curriculum 100
active sentences 100, 101
adjectives **163**
    activity 7
    cohesion between 7
    definitions of 6–7
    evaluating 7–8
    modified by adverbs 124
adverbial phrases **163**
    activities 111, 112–13
    adding to sentences 15
    introductory teaching 40
    list of 57
    placement 68, 69, 76
    prepositional phrases and 10
    statutory requirements 68

adverbs **163**
    activity 8
    assessment 158
    definitions of 7
    essential knowledge 55
    expressing time 57
    introductory teaching 68–9, 86
    list for possibility 124
    modifying adjectives 123
    modifying other adverbs 124
    National Curriculum 67
    statutory requirements 85
ambiguity **163**
    activities 138–40
    avoiding using commas and hyphens
        85, 86, 87
    big challenges 159
    essential knowledge 138
    statutory requirements 137
apostrophes **163**
    activity 22–3
    contractions and possession 21
    indicating possession 76
    National Curriculum 27

assessment
    adverbs 158
    catch up strategies 161–2
    fronted adverbials 158
    modal verbs 158
    relative clauses 158
    relative pronouns 158
    repetition not allowed 158
    sentence knowledge 157
    tense knowledge 157
    through reading 154–6
    using images for 156
    word classes 157
autobiographies 44
auxiliary verbs 5, 108, **163**

bbc.newsround
    assessment through reading 154–5
    expanded noun phrases 121–2
    fronted adverbials 71
    passive verbs 104–5, 106
    present perfect verbs 43–4
big challenges 159–60
brackets **164**
    activities 141–2, 148–9
    essential knowledge 140
    introductory teaching 86
    statutory requirements 85
Brook, Henry 155–6
Bruner, Jerome 154
bullet points
    introductory teaching 87
    punctuating 146–7
    statutory requirements 86

capital letters **164**
    introductory teaching 21–2
    National Curriculum 15
catch up strategies 161–2
Charlie and the Chocolate Factory (Dahl) 36–7
clauses **164** *see also* relative clauses;
        subordinate clauses
    embedded clauses 18
    independent clauses 35
    main clauses 18
    sentence bags 16–18
co-ordinating conjunctions 15, 32
cohesion **164**
    activities 7, 20–1
    big challenges 159
    examples in reading 52
    introductory teaching 28, 29
    National Curriculum 27
    statutory requirements 48, 87
collective nouns 4
colons **164**
    essential knowledge 143
    to introduce a list 146
    or semi-colons 144–5
    statutory requirements 86, 87
combining sentences 36
commands 15, **164**
commas **164**
    activities 77–81, 138–40, 141–2, 148–9
    direct speech 76–7
    essential knowledge 138

fronted adverbials 68–9, 76
    after fronted adverbials 77
    for lists 21
    moving clauses 77–8
    National Curriculum 27
    statutory requirements 85
common nouns 4
complex sentences 18
conjunctions **164** *see also* subordinating
        conjunctions
    activities 9–10, 33–6, 69–71
    applying in writing 37
    at the beginning of sentences 69–70
    cohesion 37
    definitions of 9
    essential knowledge 31–2, 55
    examples in reading 36–7
    expressing cause 57
    expressing time 57
    introductory teaching 32–3
    National Curriculum 15
    or prepositions 60
    types of 31
    useful conjunctions 32
context 13
countable nouns 4
Crossley-Holland, Kevin 36

Dahl, Roald 36–7
dashes **164**
    activities 141–2
    essential knowledge 140, 143
    examples in reading 145–6
    statutory requirements 85, 86, 87
derelictplaces 156
determiners **164**
    activity 12–13
    types of 12
Dippy the diplodocus 155
direct speech 76–81, **164**

embedded clauses 18
encyclopedia entries 106
exclamation marks 15, 21, 22, **164**
exclamations **164**
excuses 63–4
expanded noun phrases **164**
    activities 118–20
    applying in writing 122
    essential knowledge 47–8, 115–16
    examples in non-fiction 121–2
    examples in reading 120–1
    introductory teaching 86, 116–17
    National Curriculum 7, 115
    pronouns replacing 51
    statutory requirements 85

formal speech
    essential knowledge 89
    introductory teaching 87
    statutory requirements 85
formal writing 106
fronted adverbials **164**
    activities 70–1
    applying in writing 73

assessment 158
  commas after 77
  examples in reading 71–2
  introductory teaching 8, 68–9
  National Curriculum 27
  sentence bags 17
  statutory requirements 55
  using commas after 76
  when writing stories 72
full stops 15, 21–2, **164**
future tense 5–6

Glasser, William 153
grammar
  big challenges 159–60
  overview 153–4
  statutory requirements 27–9, 85–7, 137
Grammar for Writing 15

Hughes, Ted 10–11, 62–3
Hurricane Florence 104–5
hyphens **164**
  activities 139
  big challenges 159
  statutory requirements 85, 87

Ibbotson, Eva 113, 121, 122, 127
The Ice Palace (Swindells) 62
If I were a Book (Letria) 95
'If I were a sheep' (Wilkinson) 96
If I were in Charge of the World (Viorst) 95
If … (Smith) 95
images for assessment 156
imperative verbs 6
in or out? 35
inverted commas 77, 79, **164**
The Iron Man (Hughes) 10–11, 62–3
irregular past tense 42–3

Journey to the River Sea (Ibbotson) 121

learning 153
Letria, Jos Jorge 95
lexical verbs 5, 108
'A Lighthouse Heroine' (Brook) 155–6
lists 21
literacyshed 156

main clauses 18, **164**
mix and match 34
modal verbs **164**
  activities 125–7
  applying in writing 96, 128
  assessment 158
  essential knowledge 123–4
  examples in reading 127
  introductory teaching 86, 124–5
  National Curriculum 123
  statutory requirements 85
Morpurgo, Michael 145–6
multi-clause sentences 18

narratives 19
National Curriculum
  active/passive verbs 100

adverbs 67
apostrophes 27
capital letters 15
cohesion 27
commas 27
conjunctions 15
expanded noun phrases 7, 115
fronted adverbials 27
modal verbs 123
nouns 27, 47
perfect verbs 107
prepositional phrases 56
prepositions 56
pronouns 11, 27
question marks 15
relative clauses 130
sentences 15, 27
subjunctives 90
verbs 27
nationalgeographic 156
news headlines 44–5
nominalisation
  applying in writing 96–7
  creating 94
  examples in reading 95–6
  examples of 90
non-countable nouns 4
non-fiction
  autobiographies 44
  expanded noun phrases 121–2
  news headlines 44–5
  present perfect verbs 43–4
  relative clauses 134–5
  subjunctives 95
  types of 21
  writing 19–21
noun phrases 17
nouns **164** *see also* expanded noun phrases;
  pronouns
  activities 5, 49–52
  clarity and cohesion 27, 48
  essential knowledge 47–8
  function 3–4
  introductory teaching 48–9
  National Curriculum 27
  types of 3–5

objects **164**

paragraphs 19–20
parenthesis **164**
  activities 141, 148
  essential knowledge 140–1
  examples in reading 142
  introductory teaching 86
participles 100
passive **165**
passive sentences 101
passive verbs
  activities 102–4
  applying in writing 106
  essential knowledge 99–101
  examples in reading 104–5
  introductory teaching 87, 101–2
  statutory requirements 85

past participles 100
past tense
    introductory teaching 5–6
    irregular past tense 42–3
    or present perfect 41–2
Paver, Michelle 121
perfect progressive verbs 5–6
perfect verbs
    activities 110–13
    applying in writing 114
    essential knowledge 107–8
    examples in reading 113
    introductory teaching 86, 87, 108–10
    National Curriculum 107
    statutory requirements 85
personal pronouns 11, 49
phrases 16, **165**
place names 4
possessive apostrophes 76, 78
possessive pronouns 11, 48, 49
prepositional phrases
    examples in reading 10–11
    introductory teaching 59–60
    National Curriculum 56
prepositions **165**
    activities 59–62
    applying in writing 63–4
    cross-curricular 64
    examples in reading 62–3
    expressing cause 56, 59, 62
    expressing time 56, 57–9, 62–3
    introductory teaching 57–9
    National Curriculum 56
    or conjunctions 60
    overview 10
present participles 100
present perfect verbs
    activities 41–3
    applying in writing 44–5
    examples in reading 43–4
    examples of 6
    introductory teaching 40–1
    overview 39–40
    past tense and 41–2
    statutory requirements 27
present tense 5–6
Private Peaceful (Morpurgo) 145–6
progressive **165**
progressive verbs 5–6
pronouns **165**
    activities 49–52
    activity 11–12
    applying in writing 53–4
    clarity and cohesion 52
    essential knowledge 47–8
    examples in reading 52–3
    introductory teaching 48–9
    National Curriculum 11, 27
    personal or possessive 49–50
    personal pronouns 11, 49
    possessive pronouns 11, 48, 49
    relative pronouns 11, 18, 129, 158
    replacing expanded noun phrases 51
    too many pronouns 50–1
    types of 11

proper nouns 4, 47
punctuation **165**
    activities 22, 147–9
    big challenges 159–60
    essential knowledge 75–6
    hearing 148
    introductory teaching 21–3
    overview 153–4
    statutory requirements 27–9, 85–7, 137

question marks 15, 21, 22, **165**
questions **165**

reference chains 48, 51–2
relative clauses **165**
    activities 132–4
    applying in writing 135–6
    assessment 158
    essential knowledge 129–30
    examples in reading 134–5
    introductory teaching 86, 87, 130–2
    National Curriculum 130
    sentence bags 18
    statutory requirements 85
relative pronouns 11, 18, 129, 158
Rock Cake Raiders 73
Rosen, Michael 10
Rumbelow's Dance (Yeomans) 10
Runaround 13–14

The Secret of Platform 13 (Ibbotson) 113, 127
self-reflection 160
semi-colons **165**
    activities 148–9
    correct, incorrect or not needed 144
    essential knowledge 143
    formal writing 143–4
    or colons 144–5
    statutory requirements 86, 87
sentence bags 16–19, 157
sentences **165**
    assessment 157
    combining sentences 36
    complex sentences 18
    multi-clause sentences 18
    National Curriculum 15, 27
    single clause sentence 17
Series of Unfortunate Events (Snickett) 135
Short!: A Book of Very Short Stories
    (Crossley-Holland) 36
simple verbs 5–6
single clause sentence 17
Smith, David J 95
Snickett, Lemony 135
spiral curriculum 154
statements 15, **165**
The Story Shop! 155–6
story telling game 33–4
subjects 99, **165**
subjunctives *see also* nominalisation
    activities 93–4
    essential knowledge 89
    examples in reading 94–5
    examples of 89–90
    introductory teaching 91–2

National Curriculum 90
subjunctive form 90–1
subordinate clauses **165**
    activities 34, 77–8
    essential knowledge 129
    examples of 18
    relative clauses and 131
subordinating conjunctions
    activity 69–70
    introductory teaching 9, 15
    phrases 32
    words 32
Swindells, Robert 62

teaching others 160
tenses 157, **165**
test papers 160–1
texts 19–21

Venn diagrams 64
verb chains 17
verbs **165** *see also* modal verbs; passive verbs;
    perfect verbs
    activities 6, 41–2

applying in writing 44–5
definitions of 5
essential knowledge 39–40
examples in reading 43–4
introductory teaching 40–1
National Curriculum 27
tenses 5–6, 39
types of 5
verb forms 108
Viorst, Judith 95
vocabulary, statutory requirements 27–9,
    85–7, 137
Vulgar the Viking 73

walking the wall 35
We're Going on a Bear Hunt (Rosen) 10
Why? Encyclopedia 95–6, 105, 134–5
Wilkinson, Anne 96
Wolf Brother (Paver) 121, 122
word classes 3, 157
words bags 16
words in context 13

Yeomans, John 10

www.ingramcontent.com/pod-product-compliance
Ingram Content Group UK Ltd.
Pitfield, Milton Keynes, MK11 3LW, UK
UKHW051602281224
452811UK00001B/2